Island Base

Island Base

Ascension Island in the Falklands War

Captain Bob McQueen CBE RN

Commander British Forces Support Unit
Ascension Island

Whittles Publishing

Published by
Whittles Publishing,
Dunbeath Mains Cottages,
Dunbeath,
Caithness KW6 6EY,
Scotland, UK
www.whittlespublishing.com

Typeset by
Gwen Ord-Hume Typesetting

© 2005 R McQueen

ISBN 1-904445-18-7

Printed by Bell and Bain Ltd., Glasgow

CONTENTS

List of Contributors

Lieutenant Colonel William D Bryden USAF

Colonel Bryden served for a total of twenty-seven years in the USAF including a two-year married accompanied tour from 1981 to 1983 as the Commander of Ascension Auxiliary Airfield. He volunteered for his assignment to Ascension because he had travelled through there several years before while on an avionics test mission based on Wright Patterson Air Force Base and fell in love with the unique island. After leaving the Air Force, he worked for 15 years developing air traffic control systems for the Federal Aviation Agency (FAA) and for the UK National Air Traffic System (NATS). His last job was as Director of Lockheed Martin Air Traffic Control in the UK. He retired in 2000 and now lives in Wilmington, North Carolina where he serves on several boards for local government and charitable organizations.

Commodore Michael Clapp CB RN

Michael Clapp joined the Royal Navy in 1950 and first saw operations in the Korean War. He subsequently became an Observer in the Fleet Air Arm and commanded the first Buccaneer Mk2 Squadron at sea. He had three ship commands, one of which was during the Indonesian Confrontation when he was mentioned in despatches. He retired soon after the Falklands campaign and became a stockbroker in Devon. He is married with three children.

Captain Chris J S Craig CB DSC RN

His 34 years of Royal Navy service included 17 years as a helicopter pilot/instructor and nine appointments in command – most notably 705 and 826 Naval Air Squadrons, HMS *Monkton*, HMS *Alacrity* during the Falklands War, HMS *Avenger* and the 4th Frigate Squadron, HMS *Osprey* Naval Air Station, HMS *Drake* barracks, and Task Force Commander of all Royal Navy ships and naval aircraft afloat for the Gulf War of 1991. He has written an excellent book entitled *Call for Fire*.

Colonel Peter Hill RE

Peter Hill was commissioned into the Royal Engineers in 1963 and then took an engineering degree at Cambridge. After service in Cyprus, Germany and the UK, he specialised in construction engineering but also attended the Army Staff College. At the time of the Falklands war, he was instructing Sapper officers in the design of reinforced concrete structures and was selected to go to Ascension Island as he had both technical and staff skills. He retired from the Army in 1993 to be the Director of Estates at Oxford University.

Captain Peter Hore RN

Captain Hore served worldwide in the Royal Navy from 1962 to 2000, mostly in frigates and destroyers. He is a fluent linguist who also plays chess and sailed for the Royal Navy. During the Falklands War he was Joint Logistics Controller on Ascension Island. He has headed both the Royal Navy's Applied Research Programme and its Non-Technical Research Programme. His last appointment in uniform was as Head of Defence Studies during the British government's Strategic Defence Review, the rewriting of *British Maritime Strategy*, and the launch of a new concept of operations, the *Maritime Contribution to Joint Operations*. Peter Hore is now associate editor of *Warships International Fleet Review*, op-ed writer for *Newsday* in New York, and obituarist for the *Daily Telegraph* in London. He is the author of many reviews and articles and five books. By day he is Executive Director of the Cinema and Television Benevolent Fund, the trade charity of the film, cinema and commercial television industries.

Miss Cecilia James

Miss James' great grandfather was a gold prospector in South America, so perhaps travelling is in her genes! She is a primary teacher and has taught in the Seychelles, North Borneo and on Ascension Island. Her previous career as a Norland Nurse took her to France and South Africa. As a bit of a loner, her passions include islands, wilderness, the sea and wildlife photography. She is currently teaching sick children in a Hospital School in Plymouth, Devon.

Admiral Sir Michael Layard KCB CBE

Michael Layard retired from the Royal Navy in 1995 after some forty years service – first as a Seaman Officer, then as a fighter Pilot. He commanded the last Sea Vixen Squadron (899), HMS *Lincoln*, HMS *Cardiff* and the Royal Naval Air Station at Culdrose.

As a Rear Admiral, in 1988, he was the Fleet Air Arm Tribal Chief, Flag Officer Naval Air Command (FONAC), later to embrace all active Naval Aviation as the Flag Officer Naval Aviation (FONA). Finally he was the first combined Second Sea Lord and C-in-C Naval Home Command, on the Admiralty Board and responsible for all Royal Naval and Royal Marine personnel policy. In the Falklands War, he was the Senior Naval Officer in SS *Atlantic Conveyor*, and was awarded the CBE. He is currently involved in many projects ranging from Charities and Trusts, to School Governorships, the NHS and the Fleet Air Arm Museum.

Lieutenant Commander (SD Reg) Ernest Lord

Ernie Lord joined the RN in 1957 as a Boy Seaman and trained as a signalman at HMS *Ganges*. He transferred to the Regulating Branch and subsequently commissioned as Sub-Lieutenant in 1974. Notable jobs include service with 814 Naval Air Squadron in HMS *Hermes*, and Naval Provost Marshal at Portland and Plymouth. His last appointment was Officer in Charge Whale Island – before HMS *Excellent* was refurbished, renamed and renewed. He is married with two daughters and two grandchildren. He now works as an administrator, a gopher/dogsbody at a hospital near Southampton.

Captain Robert McQueen CBE RN

Robert McQueen joined the RN as a National Serviceman in 1952, and qualified as a Fleet Air Arm pilot in 1957. His first command was HMS *Salisbury* in 1970 and in 1974 he was promoted to Captain. He commanded HMS *Diomede* in the Icelandic Cod War before going to the MOD as Deputy Director, Naval Administrative Planning. From 1979 to 1982 he was Flag Captain to the Flag Officer Sea Training and in command of the Naval Air Station, HMS *Osprey*. In 1982 he was awarded CBE for meritorious service as Commander British Forces, Ascension Island. His last naval appointment was in command of HMS *Broadsword* and the 2nd Frigate Squadron, where he was appointed ADC to HM the Queen. After leaving the RN in 1984 he had a distinguished career in the aeronautical industry until 1994, and then occupied senior positions in a number of service charities.

Group Captain Jeremy S B Price CBE RAF Retired

Jeremy Price graduated from the RAF College Cranwell in December 1959. A tour on No 80 (Photo Reconnaissance) Squadron Canberras at RAF Bruggen was followed by a succession of tours at RAF Marham flying Valiants, Victor 1s and 2s in the air-to-air refuelling role. These flying tours were interspersed with tours at the Headquarters No 1 Group Tanker Planning Cell, the RAF Staff College and Headquarters Strike Command as air refuelling adviser to the Air Defence Staff. Promoted to Wing Commander in 1974 he returned to RAF Marham, first to command No 232 Operational Conversion Unit, training aircrew to fly and operate the Victor K2, and then No 57 Squadron during the build up of the Victor K2 tanker fleet.

After a tour at the USAF Air University, Maxwell Air Force Base, Alabama, he returned to command RAF Marham in 1981. During Operation Corporate he was detached, from April to July 1982, to Ascension Island serving as the Senior RAF Officer and then Commander British Forces Support Unit. On leaving Marham he attended the Canadian National Defence College before his appointment to the MOD as Director of Defence Commitments (UK) in 1984. He took early retirement in 1987.

Norman Shacklady Esq

Norman Shacklady joined the BBC's Engineering Division in 1950 as a Technical Assistant in the Transmitter Department, gaining engineer status in 1958. In 1981, following a number of managerial posts, he was appointed Resident Engineer in charge of the South Atlantic Relay Station (Ascension Island), a high power HF (short wave) station relaying World Service programmes to South America. He retired in 1986 as Senior Manager of all the BBC's overseas HF relay stations. In 1988, under a short term contract, he undertook a further two-year tour of Ascension Island, again as Resident Engineer.

Major General Julian H A Thompson CB OBE RM

Julian Thompson served for 34 years in the Royal Marines in many places round the world, including the Falklands War of 1982, in which his brigade carried out the initial landings and fought the majority of the land battles. After leaving the Royal Marines he was a consultant with the Insurance Brokers Alexander & Alexander (later Aon) advising on crisis management and terrorism. He is now a Visiting Professor at the Department of War Studies, King's College London, where he provides consultancy advice to companies with interests in the defence field and commercial operations in remote areas, and is Chairman of SES Strategies Ltd. He has published eight books on military historical subjects, contributed to six others, and edited one.

Commander G Anthony C Woods OBE

Tony joined the Royal Navy as a Junior Air Mechanic in 1949. He served in 738, 766 and 890 Squadrons. Following technician training, he served in 800 Squadron and HMS *Ark Royal*. Commissioned in 1964, he served in 849 and 824 Squadrons and held a number of Engineering Staff appointments. He was promoted Commander in 1979, served as SNO Ascension during the Falklands War, retired from the RN in 1985.

Acknowledgements

To all my contributors, I wish to express my gratitude for their willing, patient and enthusiastic efforts. They have given this book the benefit of a variety of different perspectives that add to its tapestry of opinion. I am particularly grateful to those like Julian Thompson and Michael Clapp who went on to win the war but were also prepared to write on the deployment and build-up phase. Contributions from the locals like Norman Shacklady and Cecilia James are a valuable part of the story. Bill Bryden's tale reflects the total cooperation which he invariably showed at the time, but not the extra encouragement and help that he has given me since. I regret not having been able to include a tale from Bernard Pauncefort, the Resident Administrator, nor a tale from the Hercules Force (the Truckies) who got on with their task without fuss and with considerable fortitude.

This book would not have come to pass without the constant encouragement of Nadya, my wife, since the day twenty-three years ago when I returned from Ascension Island. Equally, Captain Christopher Page, Head of the Naval Historical Branch, Captain Peter Hore, my right hand man during the operation who introduced the book to my publisher, Dr Keith Whittles, have been a source of great enthusiasm, encouragement and professional advice.

Unless given in one of the tales by my contributors, the opinions expressed are entirely my own and have no official standing or endorsement.

Grateful thanks are extended to Lieutenant Colonel William Bryden, Colonel Peter Hill, Admiral Sir Michael Layard, Roy Lennox, Group Captain JSB Price and RA Wilson for providing photographs.

Ministry of Defence
Old War Office, Room 231
Whitehall, London SW1A 2EU

Telephone: 020 7218 6193
Fax: 020 7218 7558
Email: cns1sl-mail@defence.mod.uk

Baroness Thatcher of Kesteven OM PC FRS wrote in her memoirs in 1993: "The significance of the Falklands War was enormous, both for Britain's self-confidence and for our standing in the world. Since the Suez fiasco in 1956, British foreign policy had been in one long retreat. The tacit assumption made by British and foreign governments alike was that our world role was doomed steadily to diminish. We had come to be seen by friends and enemies as a nation which lacked the will and capacity to defend its interests in peace, let alone in war. Victory in the Falklands changed that. Everywhere I went after the war, Britain's name meant more than it had. The war also had real importance in relations between East and West: years later I was told by a Russian general that the Soviets had been firmly convinced that we would not fight for the Falklands, and that if we did we would lose. We proved them wrong on both counts, and they did not forget the fact."

In the aftermath of the conflict whose effects Lady Thatcher summarises so well, much was written about the war, but very little about the island that was so crucial to our success. This importance was summed up unequivocally by Commodore Mike Clapp, Commander of the Amphibious Task Group, who said: 'without Ascension Island, there would have been no Operation Corporate.' This short book, a compendium written by those who were there, shows how the island was an essential stepping stone in the execution of a daring plan in response to Argentinean aggression. Captain McQueen, who commanded our forces on the Island during the war with single-minded purpose and great ability, has collected the accounts of several of the main participants.

On Ascension, lack of facilities required much improvisation in a fast changing situation. All this was accomplished with commendable dedication and humour by our armed forces, in conjunction with Americans, PANAM employees, St Helenian and other civilian occupants of this South Atlantic Island.

This book forms a small tribute to all those who were there at this historic time, and is an important piece in the jigsaw of our understanding of the history of the Falklands War.

First Sea Lord

Alan West

June 2004

Chapter 1

THE ISLAND

First discovered in 1501 by the Portuguese sailor Joao de Nova and rediscovered on Ascension Day 1503 by Alphonse d'Alburque, the island remained uninhabited until the early 19th century, when, with Napoleon exiled to nearby St Helena, the small garrison was established. In 1922 Ascension became a dependency of St Helena with the Administrator appointed by Britain. Wideawake airfield was built in World War II as a staging post between Brazil and Africa. Since 1957, it has been leased to the American government to serve their satellite and missile tracking facilities and is operated on contract by Pan American Airways. Other facilities include NASA, Cable and Wireless and the BBC.

Ascension Island is 34 square miles of the most hostile environment one can imagine. The nightmare landscape consists of volcanic ash and dust, clinker, broken rock, lava flows and frowning mounds of slag and extinct volcanoes. Newcomers to the island are struck by the jaggedness and sharpness of the rock apparently newly-blasted from a quarry, although in fact Ascension is geologically speaking, young (a few million years) so the rock has had little time to weather or be eroded. The volcanic dust is pervasive and the volcanic rock wears out shoes and tyres at a remarkable rate.

Situated at 7 ° 56´S and 14 ° 25´W in the trade winds, Ascension Island enjoys a stable climate; the temperature is about 65–70° F year-round and a prevailing south-easterly breeze at about 18 knots on 364 days of the year carries the all-pervading dust. On the coast there are some 6 inches of annual rainfall: according to the Admiralty Sailing Directions known as the Pilot, this falls in form of light showers or drizzle but, in early 1982, much of it fell in heavy tropical downpours which caused flash floods and large pools of standing water, though these quickly evaporated. In contrast, Green Mountain on the windward side of the island has some 20 inches of rain. Formerly water was stored in catchments but by 1982 these were disused. On the upper slopes of Green Mountain is a derelict farm, once successfully run by Cable and Wireless as the island's primary source of fresh meat and vegetables. Records suggested that plant colonisation of Ascension is still taking place, and may in turn bring more rain, as the early farm managers hoped. The island would be an ideal subject for botanical and agricultural study.

The highest point of the island, Green Mountain, is 2,817 feet high and is covered by small bamboo forest. When I first visited the island in 1957 in HM Yacht *Britannia*, I had not been on watch ashore but His Royal Highness Prince Philip and his party had come back and described how they had gone through a long dark tunnel and come out into fairyland. This was up Green Mountain and I was to discover later exactly what they meant. About ten acres around the top of Green Mountain contain sufficient vegetation for the farm which, in its heyday, supported 1,180 sheep and grew vegetables and fruit. The sensation of walking through the long tunnel and emerging on to the slopes of the mountain is akin to awakening in the Dorset countryside. The farm was known as the Red Lion and it is said that, during the war, an energetic aircraftsman walked up to it, went in and was asked if he wanted anything to eat and drink. After a good meal and a few beers, he asked for the bill, to be told that this was a private house and he was their guest!

The verdant appearance of Green Mountain contrasts starkly with the barrenness of the lower slopes. Some bays have beaches of marvellous soft white sand but are enclosed by sharp rocks, and all round the island the unexpected swell, strong undertow and offshore set, to say nothing of the voracious sea life (blackfish, moray eels, sharks) are a discouragement to bathing. In short, Ascension would be an ideal holiday for hay-fever suffering non-swimmers. Ascension is famous for green turtles which land on Clarence Beach to lay their eggs – to watch this and the hatching of the baby turtles is a magical experience. The island is also the breeding ground for the sooty or Wideawake tern, vast numbers of which settle for four months every year to lay and hatch their eggs. Other wildlife includes feral donkeys, goats, cats, rabbits and partridges.

Not unexpectedly Ascension went unclaimed by any nation from its discovery in 1501 until 1815. In the year of Napoleon's exile the Royal Marines garrisoned Ascension to forestall any French rescue attempts. Thus Ascension became the second most remote inhabited island in the world. From 1815 to 1922 the Admiralty administered the island, but in the latter year control passed to the Eastern Telegraph Company. During World War II and again from 1964 the Colonial Office appointed a career diplomat as Administrator, though subordinate to the Governor of St Helena. During World War II the USA obtained a lease of parts of the island and over 4,000 men were employed building and manning an airstrip. From March to July 1942 they underwent prodigies of endurance, living on 2 pints of water a day and without resupply for three and a half months. On 15th June 1942 the first landing on Ascension by aircraft was a Swordfish on anti-submarine reconnaissance flown from HMS *Archer*. Nearly inaccessible by sea, Ascension was joining the 20th century.

As a consequence of its history and its lack of water or any other natural resource, Ascension has no indigenous population and there are no claims on its territory. The British Crown owns all land, and only the Governor of St Helena may grant 'certificates to occupy'. In 1982 the residents were all employees or contractors of British companies and American agencies working on the Island, e.g. GCHQ, Cable and Wireless (C&W), BBC, PanAm, South Africa Cable (SAC), NASA, NSA, etc. The European and St Helenian workforce lived in quarters built by their employers, and the American workforce lived in quarters provided by various agencies, but administered by PanAm. Although some of this accommodation was used by British Forces, its availability could not be guaranteed. The residents lived pleasant, sociable, if precarious lives: most worked shifts, and they enjoyed two of the world's worst golf courses. The soil if irrigated is fertile and keen gardeners bought treated effluent from the sewage works to grow flowers around their temporary homes.

In April 1982 the population of Ascension Island consisted of about 1000 people, including 58 European families and 600 St Helenians, amongst whom there were some 200 schoolchildren, and about 200 American unaccompanied civilians. No one else was allowed to land on the island without permission nor to reside there unless employed by one of the companies or member of HM Forces on active service. Children on reaching 18 years of age are obliged to leave unless, exceptionally, they find employment. Pensioners must return home.

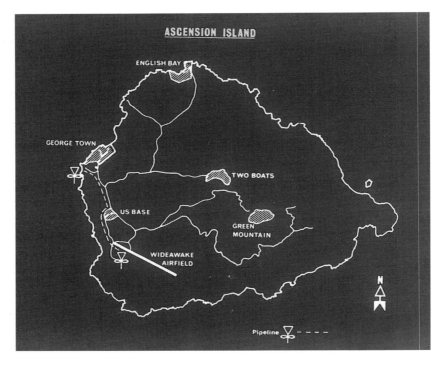

Plan of Ascension Island

The attitude of the St Helenians and the expatriates on Ascension was vital to the success of the British operations, and they were, to a man, totally loyal, enthusiastic and cooperative. Although it is invidious to mention any individual or group of islanders, special mention must be made of two groups as examples of the rest. First, the airfield staff, the fire and security men, who worked twelve-hour shifts, and second, the ever versatile Cable and Wireless maintenance men. These latter in addition to their normal duties of public works took on the initial renovation of derelict buildings and the operation of the pier head.

There is no port on Ascension and only a landing at a stone pier in Clarence Bay, on the western side of the island. An unpredictable swell in the bay ranging from 4 to 40 feet governs the use of boats in the bay and landing at the pier. The height of the swell is attested by the sand, which over the years has been thrown into Fort Thornton 200 feet above the pier. The unpredictability of the swell is rather like the Loch Ness monster – only believed by those who have seen it. While showing the view of the anchorage from Cross Hill to some VIPs, out of a flat calm sea came three rollers which swept across the bay and broke over the pier head. Minutes later the sea was flat again – the only evidence of this phenomenon was a loaded lighter which had been turned through 90°.

Much has been made of the increased air activity on Ascension (of which more later) but the success of the harbour operations deserves at least as much acclaim. Until Operation Corporate, the pier head had been used just once or twice every two months or so, and use by night was considered impracticable. However, despite the ugly sea conditions and antiquated machinery soon men and material were pouring over the pier head. For instance, the timely and cheerful response of the St Helenians and their British managers expedited the despatch of a company of Royal Marines on their way to retake South Georgia. Without this help the despatch of the first troops from Ascension would certainly have been delayed by at least twenty-four hours. Other work included, for example, the manufacture of spigots for mounting machine guns in southbound ships and helicopters. All this and much other work required individual effort far above the normal course of duty yet all went sadly unrewarded when it came to the distribution of honours after the Falklands War.

Ascension meets the sea

In 1982 the 1000 residents lived in three centres, Georgetown on the west coast, Two Boats in the centre and the American camp near Wideawake Airfield. The Americans had a commissary and a small shop plentifully supplied from the continental USA by regular Military Airlift Command (MAC) flights. The British had two shops managed by Naval Army and Air Force Institute (NAAFI) under contract to the London Users Committee (LUC), a consortium of British firms (see below). The shops and the majority of islanders were supplied by steamer at about two monthly intervals. The appearance of being a NAAFI shop would cause trouble later.

There being no airfield on St Helena, sea passage is the only link with the outside world and ship, using a small freighter, RMS *St Helena*, the only transport home for the St Helenians working on Ascension Island. British civilians could fly to UK about once a quarter using an air charter, and this was very much a feature on the residents' calendar since it brought in rare fresh produce and milk. When the air charter was stopped from taking up fuel at Ascension the consequent absence of spare space for freight was grievously missed. Also, at the beginning of Operation Corporate the small freighter, RMS *St Helena*, was due and the air charter had only recently left. In the early days of operations the fortuitously high stocks on the Island were essential to the welfare of the newly arrived British forces. The residents allowed generous access to these stocks until shortages began to appear.

The so-called American Base was much misunderstood. The very words conjure up visions of acres of runway, several choices of clubs, a large PX, and unlimited resources. The reality could not be further from this. The USAAF Auxiliary Airfield, Wideawake, just to give its full name, had a uniformed complement of one: the Base Commander, a Lieutenant Colonel, USAF. There were no other American servicemen. There is one runway and normal activity was two or three aircraft per fortnight. There was certainly no base in any operational sense.

The legal situation regarding the use of the United States auxiliary airfield at Wideawake on Ascension Island is interesting. Ascension was one of a series of British islands which the Americans had acquired the use of in the Second World War under lend-lease. There have been a number of reviews of the treaty arrangements, the latest an Agreement between the governments of Britain and the USA dated 1956. This Agreement lasted until the 20th July 1975 and 'there afterwards until one year from the day of which either Contracting Government shall give notice to the other of its intention to terminate . . .' By 1982 the treaty had expired with neither side having given notice. The Americans regarded the treaty to be fully effective while the British

RMS St Helena, the lifeline for the islanders

considered the Americans to lease parts of Ascension Island on 12 months notice: perhaps no more than a negotiating point, but also a perspective which affected the view of each Government's appropriate representative on the island. Nevertheless both parties regarded the 1956 agreement to be fully enforceable while neither had given notice. However, an exchange of notes in 1962 obliged the Americans to grant such '. . . logistic, administrative or operating facilities at the Airfield (as) are considered by the Government of the United Kingdom to be necessary in connection with its use by . . . United Kingdom military aircraft . . .' Credit must be given to the draftsman of the exchange of notes who had added the essential clause, even though the wide interpretation it would receive during 1982 could not have been foreseen.

In summary, the British disposed of their own island as a sovereign nation, there was no American operations base on Ascension, and such American facilities as the British did use were obligated by treaty.

The island is administered by a Resident Administrator whose office is in Georgetown, the capital, if it may be so called. Throughout Operation Corporate, the Administrator was to prove a great source of support. He lived in The Residency, which is the highest dwelling on the island except for the Red Lion farm and has magnificent views. Georgetown has a very attractive Anglican Church, St Anne's, houses and office buildings. In the centre is a square which, with some interesting local rules is just large enough to serve

Golf course with browns not greens

Troops resting from range practice

as a cricket pitch. The original barracks for the Royal Marine garrison was built in 1832.

Every day the Royal Marines used to have to go up Green Mountain with a mule and water cart to collect the 80 gallons of water needed for the garrison. At about half way on the journey of five miles, they stopped for a rest in the shade of two upturned boats. Since then, the other large village on the island has become known as Two Boats. On one occasion during the war, a RM Band from the Task Force 'beat the retreat' to the delight of the locals and on another, we almost beat the very skilful St Helenians at cricket with the help of a bowler who could coax unfamiliar leg breaks from the coir matting wicket.

Chapter 2

ISLAND BASES AND AIRCRAFT CARRIERS

One of the ironies of the Falklands War was that a nation which had debated the comparative values of island bases and aircraft carriers for twenty years went to war against Argentina with both an island base and two, albeit small, aircraft carriers. It was even more ironic that a naval officer was appointed in command of the island base since this concept had been championed by the Royal Air Force.

Some of the crucial advantages of Ascension Island were as a forward, intermediary airhead, a training ground for the troops and a base where ships could embark essential stores, mail and people. It is worth calling to mind that the Task Force sailed at very short notice. Some ships sailed from Gibraltar, while others had structural alterations in home ports before heading south. One came from Belize.

Being four thousand miles from the UK meant that ships had some ten days to reconsider their urgent needs and usually these were delivered to them by air to Wideawake and helicopter (Vertrep) to their flight or upper deck. Vertrep is the common expression for the transfer of stores or people by helicopter. Transferring stores by boat or lighter was a long business, even in good weather. The Amphibious Force became involved in a large redistribution of equipment; in the main, this was done by helicopter (Vertrep), landing craft utility (LCU), landing craft vehicle and personnel (LCVP) and Mexeflote/lighter. There is little doubt that this airhead concept was very much in the mind of the Commander-in-Chief both during my call on him before deployment and in his letter to the Administrator after the war, in which he says 'Ascension Island was crucial to the success of the operation'.

Equally, there is no doubt that, in spite of the very limited port facilities, the task of transferring all the urgent stores and people to ships was successful and made a major contribution to the logistic support of our seaborne forces. The Royal Air Force did sterling service in ferrying supplies and people to the airfield. As far as the Royal Navy was concerned, Ascension Island was an extremely useful facility in the right location.

In terms of aircraft facilities, the island was much better provided. Notably, a 10,000 feet runway and a large dispersal which at one point provided parking for 24 large fixed wing aircraft and on one occasion 36 helicopters. Also critical was a fuelling buoy offshore which had a pipeline to the fuel depot at Georgetown. This meant that providing a tanker was secured to the buoy, there was a constant supply of aviation fuel to the island. Thanks to the US government, this was usually the case and it is estimated that twelve and a half million gallons of fuel were transferred in this way during the campaign.

Some practical limitations to the use of the airfield, such as no taxiway and no ammunition stowage are detailed in Chapters 5 and 11, as are the ways they were overcome.

A tanker pumping fuel through the floating pipeline

The major limitation to the use of effective air power was the island's location, 3300 nautical miles from the Falklands. This meant that nearly all flights from Ascension to the war zone had to be refuelled in flight and, in the case of the Vulcan raids on Port Stanley airfield, this required a very large number (11) of Victor Tanker aircraft. In spite of the outstanding professionalism shown by everyone concerned with air-to-air refuelling and the considerable flexibility this gave, the island base was too far from the Falklands to play any significant role in achieving air superiority in the war. For example, as Nigel West says in his book *The Secret War for the Falklands*, 'although 206 Squadron was known to be flying missions down to the Exclusion Zone, in planes hastily converted for airborne refuelling it was really nothing more than a toothless tiger, because its unarmed aircraft and ancient Searchwater radar were never intended for use in the AEW role'. Enough has been written about the elaborate but uneconomic series of six Black Buck Victor raids which attempted to destroy Port Stanley airfield, to reach the conclusion that this exceptional piece of airmanship, both in its planning and execution, had a deterrent, psychological effect rather than any significant denial of the airfield's use.

Aircraft Carriers

The remarkable way in which the limited number (maximum twenty five) of Harrier aircraft achieved a mounting and eventually major but not total air superiority over a number of Argentinian attack aircraft variously estimated at 249 and 130 (Chilean estimate) has been thoroughly documented elsewhere. The superb combat skill and courage of the aircrew combined with the unique combat capability of the Harrier and the highly effective Aim 9L Sidewinder missiles to enable results totally disproportionate to the small numbers of aircraft we were able to deploy.

HMS *Invincible*, one of our two aircraft carriers, had been sold to the Royal Australian Navy as a part of Mr Nott's ill-conceived Defence Review. The small size of these two aircraft carriers limited the numbers of Harrier aircraft that could be deployed in them. This was widely recognised as witnessed by Sir (Mr at the time) Caspar Weinberger's offer to Sir Nicholas Henderson of the use of a larger American aircraft carrier. Any Airborne Early Warning (AEW) capability was totally lacking.

In terms of capability, the Royal Navy approached the Falklands War horrendously under equipped. This underlined the risks of the operation and gave even greater emphasis to the courage and resolve of the First Sea Lord, the Chief of the Defence Staff and the Prime Minister in undertaking it.

HMS Hermes at Ascension

Command and Control

In a sentence, there was too much of the former and not enough of the latter. My terms of reference were quite clear. 'You are responsible to the Chief of Defence Staff through the Vice Chief of the Defence Staff (Personnel and Logistics) (VCDS (P&L)).' At a meeting I attended in the Ministry of Defence immediately prior to my deployment, two things were agreed. The first was that tri-service numbers on the island would not be more than about two hundred and the second that I should have the power of veto on anyone sent there. Both these resolutions were broken within a fortnight.

It quickly became clear to all of us on the Island that the demand for people to come to Ascension far exceeded the supply of facilities required to support them. Among the constraints were water, accommodation (particularly aircrew standard), food, aviation fuel, aircraft parking space and bizarrely, money – we ran out.

Throughout the seventy day war, VCDS (P&L)'s staff (Staff of Chief of Personnel and Logistics) (SCPL) defended us valiantly but they were outnumbered by the fact that there was only one war and there was an over supply of people who wanted to be a part of it. These were quickly styled as 'tourists' by the Ascension locals who wondered if we 'had got the right island.' The almost complete lack of existing facilities did not feature in people's thinking in the UK. On the island, I became known as Captain One In, One Out and my first Senior Royal Air Officer (SRAFO) Group Captain Mike Tinley spent hours on the red phone persuading those commanders who were sending detachments to trim them. Early on, I met an RAF Squadron Leader Padre off a Hercules. "I have come because the Chaplain of the Royal Air Force and myself were sure that you needed a Chaplain." "That is far from the case," I replied, "we already have seven chaplains and one Bishop." (The Bishop of St Helena happened to be visiting). "You may stay if you are prepared to shift stores. We are short of people to do that," I continued. He demurred and returned forthwith to the UK in high dudgeon.

I initiated a daily meeting so that we should all know what was going on. Detachment commanders quickly understood the problem and became adept in volunteering excess personnel to be returned. This invariably led to an increasingly bitter argument with some authority in the UK. These ranged from Group Captain to Group/Command level.

With the benefit of hindsight, these problems would have been solved by having a single point of contact in the shape of a Permanent Joint Force Headquarters, such as now exists. The selection of C-in-C Fleet as Task Force Commander was a natural one and AOC 18 Group (the Maritime Operations Group) as the Air Commander flowed from that. The Joint Chiefs of Staff draft 'Lessons Learnt' concluded that 'The main problem throughout Corporate was that no information was provided by Commander Task Force's Headquarters on proposed deployments of aircraft and airmen to Ascension Island, with the result that the aircraft and personnel numbers there continually outgrew the resources. This caused much friction between the Air Staff at all levels and CBFSU.' To this, I would add that the finite limitation on numbers of aircraft able to be parked was seldom recognised as a planning factor in the more ambitious plans of the too many staffs in UK who felt obliged to contribute.

I noted, rather sadly, in my diary on the 25th May, '90% of our problems are caused by overcontrol from UK by too many agencies, usually outside their terms of reference.'

The media

Someone, I know not who, but to whom I am eternally grateful , made a decision early on that the twenty nine journalists in the Task Force would not be allowed ashore. This was not well received but was a blessing for us. We just did not have any time to deal with the distraction of looking after them. Squadron Leader McQueen, the 'other McQueen' as he was known, and I sent a message to Alastair McQueen of the *Daily Mirror* in the *Canberra* that two McQueens on one small island was a sufficiently large representation of the clan!

Air defence

Rather late in the day, 26th April, someone in UK had the bright idea that the island might be attacked by the Argentinians. This may have been caused by the Argentinian merchant ship *Rio del Plata* which was spotted by the Resident Administrator from his vantage point residence passing a few miles from the island. This led to instructions to me to 'take appropriate measures to ensure the safety of ships against the possibility that *Rio del Plata* has put ashore special purpose forces.'

I had already discussed defence of the island with Bill Bryden, the US Commander Ascension AAF and Bernard Pauncefort, the Resident Administrator. We had concluded that we were vulnerable to attack by special forces from sea or by air as well as bombing from the air by aircraft which had been refuelled in flight. However, any attack on what was regarded by South America as an American island would be political suicide since an attack on Americans on the island would be seen as a modern *Lusitania* or Pearl Harbour and would alienate Washington to an unpredictable and counterproductive degree. We assessed therefore that the risk was low.

Bernard Pauncefort, Brigadier Julian Thompson, Commander 3rd Commando Brigade and myself met to discuss the special forces threat. We agreed that we would patrol the island with helicopters and search the only area of dense vegetation with two companies of Royal Marines. We asked Composite Signals Organisation (CSO) to monitor HF band communications. Ships in the anchorage carried out defensive measures against underwater swimmers (Operation Awkward) and sailed overnight.

On 2nd May, an internal security team consisting of two army majors arrived. On 4th May, I was formally made responsible to Commander Task Force 317 (Commander-in-Chief Fleet) for the overall defence of Ascension Island. On the same day, a mobile Air Defence Radar (S259) and fifteen people to man it were airlifted in. The radar was lifted to a position on Green Mountain by Chinook helicopter on 8th and commenced operating on the

9th. A 200 mile Terminal Control Area (TCA) was announced internationally but was never enforced. The Air Defence Radar was not much use without air defence aircraft.

On 6th May, a signal from CTF 317 recognised that 'the air threat against Ascension is low and consists of covert operations by long range aircraft. Climate is mainly Visual Meteorological Conditions (VMC). Harrier GR3s adequate to cover such a threat in this climate. Use of Phantoms or Lightnings in the immediate future is ruled out due to excessive overload of Ascension facilities. 3 × GR3s will have to fulfil role. These aircraft already in position at Ascension.'

Also on 6th May, No 3 Wing RAF Regiment were flown in to guard the airfield and other key points and were joined later by No 15 Squadron. An efficient defence plan was produced by Wing Commander T T Wallis, the local defence Commander, which happily, did not need to be used.

On 17th May, for no obvious or stated reason, the threat was upgraded and at 1630 on 24th May, three F4 Phantoms from 29F Squadron arrived to replace the Harriers. This detachment proved to be an efficient and economic one.

Lord of the Flies

The problem of feeding the large numbers of service people on the island was solved by setting up three field kitchens under the very successful partnership of a Lieutenant (S) Brian Purnell, a Chief Caterer, an RAF Sergeant Simpson and a Guards Regiment Warrant Officer. The kitchens were established on the airfield, at English Bay and in Two Boats village. For some unexplained reason the field kitchen in Two Boats attracted large numbers of flies. Steps were taken to eradicate them but these were clearly insufficient for the Command Flying Medical Officer (CFMO) Strike Command. An Environmental Health Technician (EHT) was despatched to the island without my knowledge and wrote a critical report without reporting the contents to me. This led to CFMO asking for him to be assigned permanently which I refused, asking to see the report first. Clearly the Group Captain prevailed on Chief Staff Officer Logistics since a dedicated EHT was posted to my staff by MOD. This was additional to the two local doctors, four RN doctors waiting to go south, a RAF Squadron Leader and a Wing Commander who was sent to investigate aircrew fatigue! My staff had to restrain my response to this trivial but extreme example of back seat driving and persuade me not to signal the well-intentioned CFMO – 'you look after your flies and I'll look after mine!'

Flight safety

Details of some of the risks and the fact that we only had one reportable incident during the intensive air operations from Wideawake airfield are given in Chapter 11. Whilst agreeing that no small measure of luck came into the equation, it is worth outlining the make-up of my very experienced Flight Safety Team and some of the procedures that helped achieve this remarkable record. The team was Colonel Bryden USAF, Group Captain J S B Price, Mr Don Coffey, Panam Manager, Wing Commander J Morgan and Lieutenant Commander R Warden. We addressed two problems, operating fixed wing and rotary wing aircraft from the same airfield and extreme congestion on the hardstanding. With the first we benefited from previous experience at Royal Naval Air Station Culdrose. Following a tragic mid air collision when a helicopter landed on top of another taking off, it was decided that all aircraft, whether fixed or rotary, would ground or air taxi to the threshold of the duty runway for take-off and would rejoin the duty runway for a circuit or hover at the threshhold prior to taxying to dispersal. This at least meant that all aircraft, whether fixed wing or rotary wing, were going in the same direction. Pressure from CTF 317 to split fixed and rotary operations at Wideawake was resisted as we all considered that this would have brought our resupply operations to a halt. In any case there was no other piece of tarmac or concrete on the island. Without tarmac, helicopter engines ingested volcanic dust that polished them to dangerous levels.

The problem of congestion on the aircraft hardstanding was solved by treating the ramp like the deck of an aircraft carrier. Wing Commander Morgan who was the Station Engineer Officer (SENGO) of RAF Marham took control of aircraft on the ramp. Every move was planned to accommodate as many aircraft and tasks as possible up to the maximum of 24 four-jet equivalents. For instance, we were able to park the Sea Harriers waiting for *Atlantic Conveyor* on a disused road leading from the airfield, thus leaving space available for routine daily heavy Hercules and VC10 aircraft on the main hardstanding.

Foreign object damage (FOD) was a constant hazard with stores being unpacked on the upwind end of the hardstanding and a wind of 20–30 knots quite common. All five of the above-mentioned team and myself 'prosecuted' flight safety to an extent that caused some interesting moments. One of the team went to welcome a newly arrived Nimrod. "Oh yes," he said, "We do have a FOD problem", as he surreptitiously dropped a two inch nail on to the tarmac and ostentatiously picked it up. As he left, the Nimrod's crew were being organised into a FOD patrol! To go on to the hardstanding, particularly at night, was a nostalgic experience for those of us carrier-borne aviators. Equally, it was a fearsome experience to those aviators who had never experienced aircraft operations as intense as this. The Flight Safety 'team' agreed the procedures and carried them out meticulously with remarkably successful results.

London Users' Committee (LUC)

Prior to the 1960s the sole British organisation on the island was Cable and Wireless (formally the Eastern Telegraph Company) which provided all its own facilities. With the arrival of further organisations, there was the need to formalise the facilities and services. The London Users Committee, comprising senior representatives from all the four British organisations on the island was set up to jointly manage all aspects of those requirements.

This committee was represented on the island by the head of BBC (Norman Shacklock), Cable and Wireless (Ron Field) and Composite Signals Organisation (CSO) (Ray Lee). The Property Services Agency (PSA) did not have a permanent representative at the time. Common User Services such as medical and Hospital, Works Dept, Marine, Transport, two shops and the Island School were provided by Cable and Wireless. Many of my negotiations were carried out with Ron Field who was as supportive as his head office allowed in the provision of accommodation and other needs. In particular, his jetty manager (Dave Kane) proved to be an exceptionally flexible ally. Ray Lee had the extremely difficult problem that, initially, his organisation was the only conduit open to us for classified signals. He appeared regularly on the airfield with piles of signals and, in the face of such ready help, I was probably too slow in setting up alternatives to what was stretching his organisation to its limits. We already had more classified signals than we could process, many of which were unnecessary.

I am not sure how often the LUC representatives met before the war, but the Resident Administrator (Bernard Pauncefort) suggested that we meet every Saturday forenoon under his chairmanship and with the inclusion of USAF, PANAM and NASA, for the purpose of my bringing everyone up to date as far as I was able. This worked very well and several incipient problems were nipped in the bud and rumours put to rest. For example, I was able to assure them that the 1,500 empty beer barrels disembarked from Royal Fleet Auxiliary (RFA) *Fort Austin* were not 'depth charges'. They were very understanding when we asked for a ban on telephone calls overseas. I was able to give them first hand examples of classified information being passed *en clair* which would have been of great interest to our resident Russian spy ship Auxiliary Gathering Intelligence (AGI), *Zaporozhive* of the Primorye class. I also took soundings from time to time on the subject of unrestricted bathing from the Island. They continued to confirm the danger of this except in English Bay where there was a shark net and generally some supervision. Too many people had been lost to exceptionally large waves to make the risk worthwhile.

I am not sure whether these meetings would be described nowadays as 'peacekeeping' or 'peacemaking' but they were certainly worth the investment of an hour or so per week.

Chapter 3

THE LOGISTICS MIRACLE

by Peter Hore

On the morning of Friday 1st April I was told to join the Naval Emergency Advisory Group the following Monday. In the afternoon, now at home in Devon, I was told, obliquely, that I would instead be flying in a Hercules transport aircraft to Ascension Island for a task which was not revealed to me. I just had time to visit the local library and glean what I could about my destination: there were about three lines in very large gazetteer and I duly packed all my tropical white uniform.

Had political and diplomatic events turned out otherwise in the early months of 1982, Task Force 317 would have been just another group of distant ships at sea and the operational and logistic achievements of British forces on Ascension Island might have been the only British operations in the South Atlantic that year. As it was, heroic and historic events further south have eclipsed the happenings on Ascension Island and after focusing on the island for three weeks, world attention switched further south.

Like the Argentine plans, the British operation, named Corporate, commenced as an essentially naval operation and, as far as Ascension was initially concerned, in a very small way. The original signalled requirement stated that the probability existed of passing small quantities of urgently needed air-portable freight through a temporary airhead on Ascension. The response to this statement was the five officers and twenty men who arrived on the island during the first weekend of the Falklands War. They found Ascension, in the words of Admiral Fieldhouse's official despatch, to be largely devoid of all resources and possessing 'totally inadequate technical and domestic back-up'.

From this unpromising beginning the story of how Ascension grew to be the Forward Operating Base, assessed as critical and vital to the war in the South Atlantic, deserves a minor place after the many other greater achievements during that war. The rugged, remote island doubled its population in a few weeks and became briefly the busiest airfield in the world and a crowded training ground for brigade strength troops. Despite its newly found prominence, little was – and is yet – widely known of Ascension and many misconceptions persist.

The build-up of the forward operating base on Ascension from 25 officers and men during the first weekend to 800 personnel after 3 weeks and then to a peak of 1400 including transitees, happened in three overlapping phases: the initial phase and crises which developed internally on Ascension, a phase of intense operations, and a final phase of broadening tasks before the organisation was handed over in mid-July to the RAF after victory in the Falklands. The remarkable thing is that the organisation developed and functioned without written orders for several weeks, yet succeeded so well in melding together diverse units many of whose personnel had no experience of tri-service operations. Though differences in attitude and manning were revealed, force of personality, clear objectives and daily and regular briefing united the team. The rest of this chapter concentrates on the first phase of three weeks and more.

The first to arrive on Ascension on the weekend of 2nd April 1982 were not as the *Sunday Times* Insight Team reported '. . . technicians and engineers equipped with radar and traffic-control apparatus . . .', but two RAF officers from 38 Air Support Group, an officer and six men from the Royal Navy's Emergency Relief Pool to form the RN Forward Logistics Unit, a Commander and eight ratings to support naval helicopters, and a number of RN aircrew and maintainers. All other Forces came later: the senior officer was an air engineer around whom the team coalesced until the arrival of a naval Captain who had been given the title of Commander British Forces Support Unit (BFSU).

An early discovery was that although the reinforcement plan for Ascension Island had been recently revised, it had not been reviewed by the island authorities and the contents were inaccurate and largely irrelevant. A large volume of signals, received via GCHQ, had to be read through, but there was no means of replying at first, except by ordinary landline. Initially surplus accommodation was available from C&W and PanAm to feed and roof up to about 200 personnel. The pressing problems were to unload and sort pallets of stores and ammunition and to reassemble some naval helicopters which had been brought in over the first weekend of the war. The early arrivals

A jumble of stores on the crowded apron in front of a Nimrod

changed in the sunshine and set to work, and, after an 18-hour flight in a Hercules, most men then worked non-stop for 36 hours. Similar work rates continued for a long time, men working in the open quickly acquiring enviable suntans.

The organisation which developed under the command of CBFSU was threefold: first, naval operations including all rotary-wing aircraft; second, RAF operations which in particular encompassed the tremendous achievements of Transport Command; and logistics. This third function covered the internal support and administration of Ascension Island as a forward operating base, as well as, more importantly, support from Ascension to the front.

By noon on 6th April 1982 the British base had been operating for many hours continuously. Three Lynx helicopters were flying and two Wessex helicopters were preparing for ground running. In Clarence Bay the fleet auxiliary *Fort Austin* was being loaded by lighter. Hercules were arriving on regular schedule, about six or eight per day. There had been little control over the flow of men and cargo: men arriving at Lyneham simply wrote their names on an open passenger list. Units and individuals brought with them whatever equipment they or their commanders believed necessary. Stores depots diverted everything in the pipeline including ammunition to Lyneham. At Ascension this caused immediate difficulties. Some men had responded to telephone calls telling them to go South and had no orders beyond Ascension.

Others arrived days or weeks in advance of their proper ships. All had to be fed and accommodated and most were taken under command and given work. For example, the task of renovating and making ready for occupation a series of derelict huts fell to a group of artificers who were waiting to join the landing ships which were expected to arrive soon. Radio operators, destined to augment the amphibious forces, helped unload the Danish motor vessel *Aes* of stores addressed to NP89O1 (the Royal Marines garrison who had been captured in the Falklands).

The build-up in particular of ammunition was impressive and much was loaded into *Fort Austin*. After she sailed it became an urgent necessity to reduce any risks on the airfield by creating a dedicated ammunition depot. An ideal site was found in a remote valley but the only access was along a track liable to flash flooding. This led to one of many unusual demands for stores to be sent out from the UK for a pipe or similar capable of being used as a conduit under a makeshift road, 20 feet long and 4 feet in diameter and capable of withstanding a 10 ton axle weight. This arrived within two days of the demand and ammunition was soon being taken by trailers away from its unpleasant proximity to fuel, aircraft and vehicles and into some temporary shade.

A transport pool was formed by commandeering unit vehicles, as they were unloaded from Hercules. A small unit of Royal Marines ran the pool and the most conspicuous volunteer drivers were a group of young medical officers waiting to join RMS *Canberra*. When the transport pool vehicles were depleted, night raiding parties removed the fuses from parked vehicles, thus forcing the would-be possessors to ask the transport officer for help when he would promptly requisition the keys.

The PanAm accommodation was capable of taking about 200 men. A campsite at English Bay, which had been used by RAF signallers after the Second World War and by West Indian contract labour later, provided a roof for some 50 men more. Units pooled tents and rations and a field kitchen was established, manned by a RAF Field Catering Support Unit. For a while rations were one-man 24-hour type, donated by 42 Squadron RAF, requiring considerable wrist work to provide bulk meals. These contained three meals in small tins that were difficult to open with normal field kitchen equipment. Very soon however the Royal Navy had moved in refrigerated containers and landed sufficient dry food to enable a varied and interesting diet.

It is claimed that the airfield at Wideawake became the busiest airfield in the world. It is true that on one day in April Wideawake logged more aircraft movements than Chicago O'Hare International Airport, a fact which was

Joint service catering staff

established by an anonymous telephone call to Chicago itself. It is also true that until at least early June helicopter movements outnumbered fixed wing movements by a ratio of over 5 to 1. The helicopters came from visiting warships of course, and from the newly resident Wessex Vs of D Flight 845 Naval Air Squadron. Particular credit is due to the youthful naval pilots who flew more hours in the early days of April than they might have expected in a year of peacetime activity.

Initially works activity on the Island was carried out by C&W, augmented by naval ratings awaiting ships southbound. When it was recognised that the number of works tasks was multiplying geometrically with the flood of men and units, the Royal Engineers, an officer and some 40 men arrived. They were a very impressive team. Their most obvious feat was laying a temporary pipeline from the fuel farm in Clarence Bay to the airfield, but many other vital jobs were also accomplished. They commissioned a desalination plant to supplement the island's meagre supplies of fresh water, renewed the sewage system at English Bay, erected portable buildings, organised enough portable power supplies for a small sized village and all the while continued the work of surveying and renovating derelict buildings. Nor did they allow themselves much rest, but as soon as any opportunity arose they took up community projects like repairing the old bridges and paths on Green Mountain.

Aircraft parked on the apron

Fuel, in particular aviation spirit, was a persistent problem. Fortunately the Island's stocks for normal consumption were relatively large, but the frequent launch of large flights of aircraft necessary to support Vulcans and Victors on operations far south soon depleted reserves. A continual train of oil tankers was necessary in Clarence Bay but the fuel pumped ashore from these ships required time to settle. A new tank farm of fabric pillows at Wideawake and a fleet of bowsers increased reserves, but fuel always required careful management.

Control over the flow of personnel onto Ascension eventually became a pressing and major task. Men and their equipment continued to arrive unannounced and though sent with the best will in the world, there were never sufficient resources on the island to cater for and accommodate everyone. Their administration and the enforcement of discipline requires disparate skills which in the Army and RAF require distinct and separate trades, but in the Royal Navy are carried out by Masters of Arms and their Regulators. So it was, that when these tasks continued to grow, a small team of one officer and six Regulators were sent for. They arrived complete with a patrol wagon and quickly made themselves familiar and well-known, and discharged their varied duties with great tact and efficiency.

The two shops on Ascension were run by NAAFI under contract to the London Users Committee. The manager was seconded from NAAFI, the staff wore NAAFI coveralls, and the price labels and packaging were NAAFI. Only the prices did not follow this pattern but instead reflected the high cost of freighting goods to Ascension. The periodic supply ship did call in the middle of April, and generously the LUC allowed British forces to use the shops, there being no other source of nutty, tobacco, soft drinks, etc, but when eventually these began to run out the shops were reluctantly closed to British forces. The price differential and the closing of the shops caused much resentment and misunderstanding by servicemen. Soon however, the Expeditionary Force Institute (EFI), a uniformed branch of NAAFI previously unknown to most, arrived to establish a third shop in a disused bakery, at prices more familiar to soldiers and airmen from British forces in Germany. It still left the problem that the forces had seriously depleted the islanders' stocks of even the humblest item which they might reasonably expect to find in their corner shop. Further, by drinking and eating in the private clubs which had been hospitably opened to them, British servicemen were continuing, albeit indirectly, to live off the land. This situation was, in its turn relieved when, after some bureaucratic delay in London, space and free freight was approved for a weekly re-supply to the civilians on the island.

However, the supply ship, RMS *St Helena* had also featured in every islanders' plan for shipping heavy luggage, receiving seamail and returning to the island of St Helena (which has no airport). The news that her owners had chartered her to the Ministry of Defence MOD was a great blow to civilian morale. Since CBFSU had not been told in advance of this requisition, we were unable to plan for it and soothe the locals about the decision. The contractor for shipping to and from Ascension and St Helena eventually found two much smaller and in many respects inadequate ships. Lack of awareness of the consequences of diverting *St Helena* from her normal trade not only led to MV *Stena Inspector* and HMS *Dumbarton Castle* being diverted from operational tasks to carry civilian passengers between the islands of St Helena and Ascension: it also, of course, prejudiced the good community relations upon which the success of British operations was founded.

From the beginning, concern for the environment, including the breeding grounds for the rare fauna on the island loomed large in the plans for a logistics base, and for training. Accordingly, during the troop training phase on Ascension, care was taken to minimise damage. Helicopter flight paths over nesting areas were discouraged; Boatswain Bird Island, the home of thousands of seabirds, was not used for naval gunfire practice and only one

Re-equipping survivors of HMS Sheffield and Galahad

beach was used for amphibious landings. Fortunately the most popular beaches for turtles were also the least suitable for boat traffic of any sort. The sooty terns nested and bred amongst the clinker, in 'fairs', their only enemy the feral cats once imported to exterminate the rats which man had accidentally introduced. Sadly, the cats found the birds to be easier prey, but when ranges were needed to zero weapons, one good effect in 1982 was that the presence of man and the sound of small arms and missile fire scared off the cats from the fairs, but seemingly failed to disturb the birds very much.

Amongst many other tasks for which the BFSU planned and prepared were the reception of prisoners of war, the hospitalisation and evacuation of casualties, the handling of large numbers of transitees and the care of survivors. Many of these tasks eventually related to later phases, but the first and most significant was the reception of survivors from HMS *Sheffield*. The uniforms which the *Sheffield* survivors wore at Lyneham were issued at Ascension, where they had been measured by a Chinese tailor landed from HMS *Exeter*, and they were also paid and fed. Thanks once more to the generosity of the civilian community, most were cared for in small parties in peoples' homes until their flight departures, which had obviously been timed to meet the deadlines of the evening news programmes in the UK.

Eventually the arrangements for evacuees was so smooth that they were even given a chance to buy 'duty frees' from an EFI shop.

Everything was a learning process. The same principles and processes which had been developed for the evacuation of survivors could be applied to the repatriation of prisoners of war, except these were flown out in the dead of night. Every prisoner of war was photographed, and while prisoners were on the airfield lighting was arranged so they could gather no intelligence. Someone too had to read the Geneva conventions, in English and in Spanish, to make sure we knew what we doing.

Ascension has been described in one of the histories of the Falklands War as 'the hub of the greatest British logistic operation since 1945'. Most operations of this size have their own fully structured organisation for logistic support from the outset. There was no such structure on Ascension Island, where the arrangements grew pragmatically. They were however no less successful, as these few paragraphs dealing with some specific problems which emerged and how they were handled, have shown. Most were unique, requiring initiative and innovative skills to solve, all qualities that the various British Forces proved they possessed in full.

Chapter 4

NAVAL PARTY 1222 – REBUILDING HELICOPTERS AND MOVING STORES/PEOPLE

Naval Party 1222 was born on 4th April and arrived on Ascension Island on 6th April. It was commanded with great determination and common sense by Commander GAC Woods OBE Royal Navy, an Air Engineer Officer. The task was to be the forward logistic support base for ships of the task force as they moved south. NP 1222 was to receive personnel, stores, equipment, ammunition and helicopters flown out from UK by RAF and commercial transport aircraft, and to arrange for their transhipment south.

On arrival, they were confronted by a mountain of unsorted stores and a number of helicopters in bits. The first helicopters, three Lynx for RFA *Fort Austin* were already being reassembled by a small advance team, and one had been check flown. The first pair of Wessex 5 aircraft arrived on the 6th and were operational within 36 hours. A total of ten helicopters were assembled and made operational in April and a further eight in May. Later, two Lynx disembarked to Ascension for disassembly before being flown to UK.

In the wings, two Petty Officers arrived to carry out a crucial modification programme on nine Army Gazelle helicopters before they went south. The airhead resembled a Naval Aircraft Support Unit, if not a Naval Aircraft Repair Yard.

Various redeployments of helicopters meant that the resident helicopter force usually consisted of two Wessex 5s, a Chinook and either a Sea King Mk4 or Mk3.

After a while it became obvious that VC10s were happier overnight stopping at Dakar and this relieved the congestion on the apron as well as the accommodation. The task continued to increase. On 21st April we had a major Vertrep for *Fort Austin*. Our total for that day was 300 Vertreps consisting of 300 passengers and 400,000 lbs of freight.

Stores

It is recorded that some sixteen million pounds of freight and 6,000 passengers were despatched by air to Ascension Island between 2nd April and 11th July.

Responsible for this task was the indomitable Commander (Supply) Peter Hore, whose influence on the smooth flow of the operation was unruffled and benign. In the first few days the air mechanics and anyone else who was

Special delivery of stores by Vertrep

available assisted two stores ratings to sort the stores and load the helicopter nets, but this task was soon taken over by a Principal Stores and Transport Officer (Naval) (PSTO(N)) stores party under the charge of Mr R Baldwin who arrived complete with fork lift trucks. They were joined later by Army personnel. The team received and sorted stores as they arrived and rearranged them in lanes on the south-east side of the apron, according to destination, ready for loading into helicopter nets.

Many passengers in transit were flown out to the ships in the bay to help speed up the loading process. It was not always appreciated that Ascension was only a transit base for stores and equipment going south. Packages could only be identified by the Airway Bill number and movement priority: their contents were not indicated. 95% of all stores arriving in April, May and June were movement priority 01 – filing cabinets, folding chairs, ironing boards (recognizable by their shape), the lot.

An observant VC10 loadmistress will long be remembered for her diligence in noticing and obeying the warning notice REMOVE BEFORE FLIGHT on the safety pins fitted to the consignment of Skua missiles being loaded at Brize Norton. Fortunately she remembered to hand over the pins on arrival at Ascension.

Cunning and devious tricks were often necessary to persuade ship's Captains to accept more freight to go south than they really had room for. Holding their mail until last ensured that their decks remained open and that (most of) the helicopter nets had been returned. The day came when the Captain of a stately merchantman broke radio silence with "May I remind you that this is a passenger liner and not a bloody freighter".

Unsung heroes

There were many of these and I have already mentioned Mr Bob Baldwin and his Director General Stores and Transport (DGST(N)) team who slaved endlessly to cope with the mountains of stores. Also seen on a fork lift truck was Mr Don Coffey, the Panam manager, who was heard to say "You goddammed limeys are going to win this something something war in spite of yourselves!" But pride of place must go to Warrant Officer First Class (WO1) R G Randall MBE of the Royal Engineers Postal and Courier Service, who almost singlehandedly collected, sorted and dispatched two tons of airmail daily and 1000 parcels each week. The immense value of regular mail to the morale of the forces down south cannot be overstated.

RE postal detachment – vital in maintaining morale

Chapter 5

OPERATION BLACK BUCK

by J S B Price

Group Captain J S B Price, CBE, who as Senior RAF Officer, was in charge of the planning of these outstanding Air to Air Refuelling operations. No one was better qualified than Jeremy for this role. He had spent a large part of his RAF career in flight refuelling and Victors. I had first met him in 1967 when he masterminded my Sea Vixen Squadron's deployment to Cyprus. He was joined on 29th April by Air Vice Marshall G A Chesworth, who proved to be helpful in arranging for the MOD to clear the operation with the Chairman of Cable and Wireless, although it was never explained why this should have become necessary.

Wideawake – the airfield

The geography of the airfield and its facilities had a significant impact on air operations. In particular, these were the access to the runway, the nature of the surrounding areas, the supply of aviation fuel, the lack of permanent buildings, and the routine needs of our PanAm and USAF hosts which had to be taken into account.

There is only one access from the parking area to the threshold of runway 14 for the launch of multi-aircraft formations. If the wind direction had required the use of runway 32 it would have been impossible to launch the formations of aircraft required for refuelling operations, and in particular the bombing operations against Port Stanley airfield (codenamed Black Buck), because there is no taxiway and all aircraft would have had to backtrack on the runway itself. Fortunately the prevailing wind throughout Operation Corporate favoured runway 14.

The pervasive volcanic dust of the surrounding areas dictated how aircraft were arranged on the apron and the intervals between take-offs on the runway. Care was needed to avoid the jet exhaust of one aircraft blowing debris into the intakes of another. The operating areas were swept continually, but even so, taxying power was enough to vacuum debris from the surface into the engine intakes; in a short time, the engine compressor blades developed a mirror like finish. An early priority was the delivery of a 'Lacre' mechanical sweeper to supplement the hard pressed Panam sweeper vehicle. The two vehicles worked ceaselessly but it was a case of King Canute trying to turn back the tide! The surface of the parking apron was part concrete and part tarmac. The tarmac areas soon showed the degrading effects of fuel spillage causing softening. Even partially refuelled Victor aircraft tended to settle into the softened surface and, to reduce the amount of power needed to get a fully laden stationary aircraft moving, they were routinely 'tugged' a few feet out of their holes before engine start. It was clear that tarmac surfaces would require attention if the intensity of operations continued for an extended period but during the period of hostilities these areas withstood the wear and tear.

Fuel

The bulk fuel installation (BFI) is some 3½ miles from the airfield. Aviation fuel was supplied by US Sealift Command tankers discharging their cargo through a floating pipeline to the bfi. Initially the fuel was transported by road to 'ready use' tanks on the airfield. The critical link in the supply train was the speed at which the fuel bowser trucks could be loaded and driven from Georgetown to Wideawake. Although 12 RAF bowsers were imported to supplement the Panam fleet, the bfi could dispense fuel to only one bowser at a time and this system was under continual pressure to meet the fuel flow requirements at the airhead. One unforeseen problem was the very high rate of tyre wear caused by the extremely abrasive surface of the linking road; 3000 miles was a useful life. In late April the fuel supply to the airhead improved when, in a matter of days, the Royal Engineers assembled and commissioned a temporary pipeline from the bfi to the airfield 'ready use' tanks where fabric pillow tanks were installed to increase storage capacity. Although the pipeline needed a watchful eye on it 24 hours a day and the repeated filling of the pillow tanks accelerated wear and caused leakages, the system significantly improved fuel availability at Wideawake and reduced the time taken to refuel aircraft for their next mission. At the end of hostilities, air operations from Ascension had consumed 12½ million US gallons of aviation fuel.

Fabric fuel tanks at Wideawake airfield

Detachment support

Permanent buildings were few; the main ones being the nose hangar and the PanAm ground equipment building. There was no alternative but to accommodate all detachment support under canvas or in inflatable buildings, the latter providing a 'clean', or at least a 'cleaner', environment for the storage and servicing of sensitive equipment. Sunlight, wind and abrasive volcanic dust soon took their toll while exposure to UV radiation degraded material and equipment serviceability.

PanAm requirements

With the hectic pace of events it was easy to overlook the needs of our hosts who went out of their way to assist in every way they could. Their knowledge and experience of managing the airfield proved invaluable and greatly speeded up the bedding-in process. The tempo of the build up together with frequency of helicopter and fixed-wing operations for the airfield manned for only 285 movements a year caught the residents by surprise. The PanAm air traffic controllers of whom there were only two for the first month did a magnificent job. Frequent, sometimes hourly, meetings kept relations on an even keel. On an already overcrowded parking apron, the unannounced arrival of an aircraft caused consternation and a rapid reshuffling of airframes to make room for the new arrival. Special arrangements were needed to cope with a visiting C-5 Galaxy; the Victors were crammed together in a corner creating the impression of a junkyard. Our hosts were not at war and, until General Alexander Haig's attempts at mediation ceased around 24th April, some practices such as the 'hot refuelling' of helicopters (refuelling with engines running) were prohibited on safety grounds. This restriction slowed the transhipment of personnel and material from the airhead to ships of the task force. Once the shuttle diplomacy had ended we were left to our own devices much to the relief of the helicopter operators.

With the augmentation of existing facilities and the outstanding co-operation of the resident population, Ascension successfully provided the logistic and administrative support for the operational forces deployed to the island and in the South Atlantic.

Air-to-air refuelling
Four Victor tankers landed at Wideawake on 18th April and by the following day the number had risen to nine. Initially these were the only available aircraft able to penetrate the sea areas around South Georgia and the Falklands. Three maritime radar reconnaissance (MRR) missions were flown on the 19th, 22nd and 24th April. Once an aircraft reached the task area it had insufficient fuel to complete the reconnaissance and recover to Ascension so it was planned to return via a rendezvous abeam Rio de Janeiro, positioned to provide a suitable diversion airfield should either the rendezvous or refuelling fail. For the recovery, a Nimrod was launched from Wideawake to provide assistance for the join-up at the rendezvous. The Nimrod was followed by a recovery wave of 4 tankers to position 2 'topped-up' Victors at the rendezvous, the second as a backup should there be a last minute hitch with the primary tanker's refuelling equipment. This procedure formed the basis for the recovery of subsequent Vulcan and Nimrod missions.

Black Buck 1 and the following Vulcan missions up to Black Buck 6 have been well documented, as were the early problems associated with the Vulcan's uncertain fuel consumption, the primary Vulcan's failure to pressurise and the consequences of the broken probe at the final tanker/tanker refuelling resulting in both Victors flying further south than planned. The final Victor/Victor refuel was planned so any excess fuel was passed to the 'long slot' tanker having responsibility of refuelling the Vulcan for the last time.

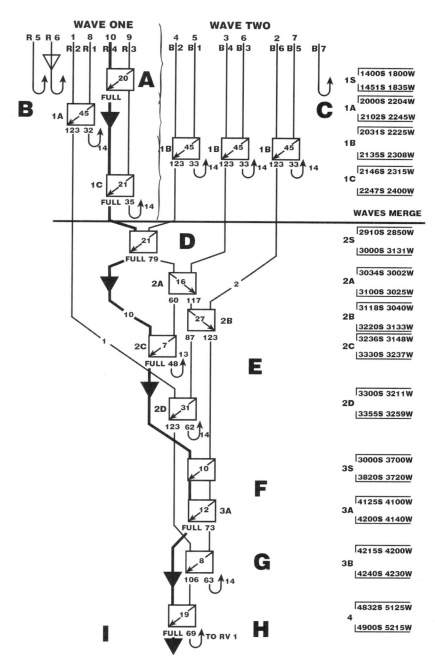

Unfortunately, while this Victor/Victor transfer was in progress the formation ran into severe air turbulence; the turbulence caused the refuelling hose to whip and break the receiving Victor's probe. The two aircraft had to swap roles but all the time the aircraft were consuming fuel and proceeding further and further south: the end result was that the tanker now providing the Vulcan's final top up had less fuel than planned. In consequence, once the Vulcan had received the quantity of fuel necessary to complete its mission the Victor had insufficient fuel to recover to Ascension, indeed it was calculated that it would run out of fuel some 400 nautical miles south of the island. The aircraft captain could not inform the operations desk at Ascension of his dilemma because, so as not to jeopardise the Vulcan's mission, he had to maintain radio silence until the codeword for the successful completion of the Vulcan raid had been received. Once operations at Ascension knew the situation two tankers were launched to head south and rendezvous with the incoming Victor: this was achieved some 600 nautical miles south of Ascension. The fuel transfer was successful and the 'long slot' tanker landed safely 14 hours 5 minutes after take off.

The planning for the Victor Maritime Radar Reconnaissance (MRR) missions was relatively straightforward compared with the challenge of devising an air-to-air refuelling plan to get the Vulcan, with its full bomb load, to Port Stanley and then recover it to Ascension. Today, I feel sure some sort of computer programme would be used for the intricate calculations, but in 1982 the plan, as one of the planners explained with a wry smile, was worked out using an electronic pocket calculator bought for £4.95 in Swaffham market. The 'number crunching' for such a complex plan was an achievement in itself and the challenge was then how best to present the mass of information. Although tanker crews were assigned a specific role in the formation, it was vital that every crew had all the necessary information readily available to switch to another position should a tanker become unserviceable for any reason. It was immediately clear that the accepted air-to-air refuelling brief, presented in 'book' form, was impractical. The solution was a stroke of brilliance, the 'spaghetti' diagram as it became affectionately known. I have chosen to show you the Black Buck 2 diagram because it incorporates the lessons learned from Black Buck 1.

It presents the mass of information on a single sheet of paper: a crew could see exactly what was required at any stage of the mission and in any formation position. With hindsight, the diagram seems to represent the obvious solution but at the time it was a major innovation.

In addition to the refuelling plan every crew had to carry a fistful of flight plans and other briefing material: all this presented a major production

Delta-wing Vulcan returning from bombing Port Stanley runway

problem. An urgent request for a copying machine was sent to Marham and there was an audible sigh of relief when it arrived at the tanker operations tent.

The outbound formation consisted of 11 Victors, including 2 airborne reserves (R5 & B7) plus the primary Vulcan (R4) and its airborne reserve (R6). At 2300 hours, in radio silence, the aircraft took off at one-minute intervals, the last aircraft leaving the runway 12 minutes after the first. At cruising altitude this represented a separation of some 85 nautical miles between the first and the last. In the early planning stages the planners envisaged a racetrack at the top of climb to allow later aircraft to catch up but it soon became clear such a procedure consumed too much fuel and it was discarded. After much pencil sucking, the formation was split into two waves. Initially the two waves proceeded as independent elements, each element joining up through speed adjustment by the lead aircraft. To enable the second wave to catch up it was planned to fly 4000 feet higher than the first wave, giving it a higher true airspeed while flying at the most economical indicated airspeed. Air-to-air Tacan range equipment between the lead aircraft of each wave provided an indication of the closing rate. The remnants of the two waves merged some 2 hours south of Ascension.

Examining the plan in more detail:

1. The principle was to move optimum quantities of fuel as far as possible down track while matching the tanker's disposable fuel with the void in the receiver's tanks.

2. The latitudes/longitudes on the right-hand side designate the start and end of each fuel transfer. The transfers 1S, 2S and 3S were amendments incorporated after the experience gained from Black Buck 1.

3. The first fuel transfer to the Vulcan (a) was to test the Vulcan's fuel system before the reserve Vulcan and its associated tanker (b) returned to Ascension.

4. The reserve tanker (c) remained with wave two until the tanker/tanker transfers at refuel 1b were complete.

5. At (d) two refuels 1c and 2s. The figure in box 1c shows the tanker transferring 21,000 lbs to the Vulcan – at the end of the transfer the Vulcan is full, the tanker has 35,000 lbs remaining and an estimated 14,000 lbs at top of descent for recovery to Ascension. At 2s – the tanker again transfers 21,000 lbs to the Vulcan, the Vulcan is full and the tanker has 79,000 lbs remaining.

6. The small quantities of fuel transferred to the Vulcan and the tanker/tanker transfers at (e) and (f) applied the principle of making maximum use of the available fuel and maintained the Vulcan's ability to recover to Ascension for as long as possible.

7. The final tanker/tanker refuel (g) was planned so that any excess fuel in tanker blue 6 was passed to the 'long slot' tanker before blue 6 turned for Ascension.

8. After the final tanker/Vulcan transfer (h) the tanker turned for the RV abeam Rio de Janeiro. The Vulcan (a) continued southwards descending to low level approximately 300 nautical miles north of Port Stanley. After the attack the Vulcan returned to Ascension via the Rio RV, the route planned to be outside mainland radar range. Two waves of 3 tankers separated by approximately 1½ hours, together with a supporting Nimrod, were launched to the Rio RV to meet the returning long-slot tanker and the Vulcan.

For Black Buck 1 the 'lone' Vulcan was airborne for 16 hours 2 minutes, the long slot tanker for 14 hours 5 minutes while the total Victor hours flown were 105 hours 25 minutes. Outbound and inbound the Victors uplifted just under 2 million pounds of fuel, that is a quarter of a million imperial gallons; the Vulcan received 7% of the total and 20% was transferred between the Victors – by the final outbound refuel to the Vulcan the fuel it received had passed through 5 different tankers.

Air refuelling proved itself as a force extender and throughout Operation Corporate distance records were being set and broken. The Victor tankers,

Shore-to-ship transfer; Victor refueller tankers in the background

Vulcans, Nimrods, Hercules, Harriers, Sea Harriers and Phantoms flew further than at any time in their operational life. The flexibility of air power was shown in abundance by planners, engineers, suppliers and, of course, aircrew.

Chapter 6

A Ship's Tale, HMS *Alacrity*

by Captain C J S Craig OBE DSC, Royal Navy

It was 0323 on the morning of 2nd April 1982. My sleep was deep and the duty signalman's shake unwelcome: HMS *Alacrity* had only come to single anchor in Portland Harbour but three hours earlier, following two weeks of constant weapon training. Rubbing the sleep from my eyes, I sighed and scanned the signal thrust before me. Though full realisation came slow, the message was unambiguous – Their Lordships required me to cancel the planned routine supersession of myself as captain, sail my ship immediately, ready her for a long absence and combat, then take her 8,000 miles south to the Falkland Islands. Where the hell were they?

At a watery first light on 5th April, following breakneck storing and ammunitioning in Plymouth, we led *Antelope* down the Hamoaze and off to war. Despite the tumult and acclaim in Portsmouth for our departing carriers *Hermes* and *Invincible* and although the British media was in full xenophobic swing, not a head turned on the Torpoint Ferry as we passed. The rattle of sabres had clearly not reached Devonport.

The two sleek frigates slipped past Mount Edgecombe, out through the narrows, beneath the rain-soaked shadow of Drake's Island and on for the open sea. Generations of naval tradition were going with us and national expectation was our spur. Mournful blasts of our sirens as we completed the final turn echoed flatly back through the dockyard and up across the sodden hillside to stately Admiralty House. It was our goodbye; and for *Antelope* – it was to be her last.

Overnight we joined the carriers and auxiliaries in dense fog off the Scillies. After three remarkable days of intense activity in dockyards, bases and stores depots, the heart of the Task Force was now established – and pulsing steadily southward. An unusually benign Biscay came and went; then the European landmass faded from our radars. Soon we experienced our first semi-tropical weather but there was no chance for enjoyment, as all ships drilled their people and readied their equipment. On our bridge-wing, the navigator gathered small teams of officers and senior ratings, all frowning gloomily as they resumed their sun-sights and star-sights. A neat little line of crosses started inching across the chart, soon to lead us deep into the storm-tossed waters of the South Atlantic.

On the 9th April we were off Madeira, on the following day – the Canaries. We imagined and envied the hedonistic pleasure-seekers ashore whilst we increased the tempo of damage control drills to ready everyone for the worst. But there were some in the Task Force softened by many years of peace who still saw this as no more than comic opera: a blast on the trumpet and those swarthy Argentinians would soon scuttle home and relinquish 'our Islands'. Some hardening of attitudes was necessary to banish complacency. For my part, I had the names of four Argentinian warships painted on our Exocet launchers and started preaching aggressively to my ship's company but, when we were just short of Ascension, Admiral Sandy Woodward decided it was time to do it his way and what an inspired move it was. He ordered a massive firepower demonstration – for ourselves alone. Ships streamed splash targets which the Harriers blew to pieces with rocket, cannon, and practice bomb, whilst all gunships fired off combined broadsides of large calibre ammunition. With the air full of cordite and ships bucking under the recoil, the Task Group came to life and the Atlantic reverberated with our pugnacity. It had been a clever piece of psychology and it lit a fire in us all.

Suitably elated myself, I obtained approval from *Hermes* to close her from right ahead to regain my station. Our 3,200 tons and 360 foot length left a mountainous wake as we flashed close down her starboard side at a combined closing speed of more than 60 miles per hour. A bored chef ditching the gash (throwing away the refuse) from the carrier's quarterdeck did not even raise his head. The giant grey ship stayed implacably indifferent to the Jack Russell terrier snarling past. Suitably deflated, I came back to heel.

Then, in the hazy light of dawn on 16th April, we first saw Ascension. A carbuncle of a place lying on a latitude of eight degrees south, the red brown volcanic ash rises 18,000 feet from the ocean floor, offering only its final 2,800 foot above sea level. The result of an eruption from the mid Atlantic ridge, this was to be our last landfall for nine weeks and although there was to be no shore leave for any of us, the island was at least a contrast to the empty horizon. Thus it almost made a beautiful sight although few of us had any real appreciation of the huge significance that this tiny island would assume in the coming struggle.

The Carrier Group, by now comprising more than 20 ships, anchored in Clarence Bay at lunchtime and, despite the fair weather, I put out plenty of anchor cable and kept the ship at one hour's notice for sea. Resupply by helicopter commenced immediately and was a stunning sight. Reminiscent of Francis Ford Coppola's epic Vietnam film, *Apocalypse Now*, for hour after hour, Sea Kings delivered scores of underslung loads to our flight deck or forecastle whilst, high above the locust cloud, a continuous stream of fixed wing aircraft landed and departed the island runway. C130 Hercules, RAF VC10s and various chartered aircraft for once ensured that Wideawake Airfield fully lived up to its name.

The frenzied activity aloft was mirrored in the grey hulls anchored below. Preparations that had commenced immediately on leaving UK could now be intensified as ship's organisations relaxed from transit watch-keeping. Aircraft were re-painted drab wartime livery and ship's side numbers were obscured. Home comforts disappeared, plastic panels that might shatter into a thousand razor-sharp fragments were stripped out and all carpets and fabrics disappeared into storerooms. Blindfold escape drills proved that abandoning a darkened warship – even one that had been your home for a couple of years – can be infernally difficult.

Hong Kong enlisted laundrymen and NAAFI personnel in all ships were offered the chance to disembark. Many stayed, some to cover themselves with credit in the bloody weeks that lay ahead. Spanish speaking interpreters had been flown out to us, as had the brand new Sea Skua missiles for our Lynx helicopter. Signal intelligence covered everything from Argentinian attack aircraft, through army boots, to the vagaries of the Latin temperament. Missile systems were endlessly tested, gun mountings greased and re-greased, high explosive ammunition prepared – we ticked off item after item on our 'Preps for War' list. The Task Group was humming.

In the midst of the bedlam, we received our first mail since leaving; a service which was to flow uninterrupted via Ascension for the next two months. For now, many of the letters were emotional as loved ones tried to re-express snatched farewells from two weeks earlier. But many missives came from unknowns who had simply lifted our name from the papers to wish us success and safety. There was no disguising their desire to stiffen our sinews for what was seen as a glamorous endeavour – the body bags were yet to be seen on television. From these sober and inspiring messages we derived much strength. Such letters were displayed on notice boards and several sailors acquired instant pen pals, particularly via the scented sheets from young 'virgins' promising to stiffen more than their sinews on completion of the great adventure. There were many benefits in heading for a 'Just' war, fully supported by the nation.

High level visitors to the Flagship included Commander-in-Chief Fleet, Admiral John Fieldhouse the overall Task Force Commander, from his underground headquarters at Northwood. Ultimately accountable to the Ministry of Defence, he would be providing strategic direction to the Task Group Commander, Admiral Woodward. He was accompanied by the designate Land Force Commander, Major General Jeremy Moore, Royal Marines.

Master war plans were being finalised. The Task Force was to split into five groups: the carriers, replenishment vessels and escorts; the amphibious ships and escorts; HMS *Brilliant* to lead a fast advance probe; the Paraquat force intended to retrieve South Georgia; and the already deployed nuclear submarines to deter Argentinian surface ships and reconnoitre their ports. In the hope that South Georgia would first be regained, the three remaining objectives for the Falkland Islands were to impose sea blockade; then to establish sea and air supremacy; and finally to regain possession. Meanwhile, diplomatic efforts were to continue unabated in pursuit of a peaceful solution – but were not to slow military preparations. The eventual Falkland landing location in San Carlos was also selected that day, though we escort COs were only made aware of the intended beachhead one month later. 'Need to Know' was the governing rule and, at that stage, *Alacrity* had no such need.

The Amphibious Group started lumbering into the anchorage on 17th April and clattering hordes of helicopters re commenced their swarming. Commodore Mike Clapp in *Fearless* would keep his force behind for the moment, to store and allow the embarked military the chance to continue their physical conditioning. He also retained half the Commando Sea King helicopters from *Hermes* to assist with the endless distribution of stores and rehearsing for invasion.

The carrier group sailed the next day with 3,300 miles to go to our destination. *Invincible* followed later that evening, having only arrived at Ascension after we had sailed due to her gearing defect delays. She had only six hours of storing and respite.

Soon after departure, jittery nerves were given an outlet. Intelligence had rightly cautioned us that Ascension was so obvious and significant a British advance base, that Argentinian submarines might try a daring pre-emption to sink one of our ships. It all started with a 'confident' periscope sighting by *Olmeda* and then became a farce of overreaction, as several ships gained very real high speed sonar contacts and proceeded to hurtle around the ocean growling and snorting, tracking the intruders. Thankfully the delicately poised international situation temporarily denied us the use of our anti submarine munitions, otherwise we would have had none left by the end of the day. Hour after hour it went on, with fleeting detection following fleeting detection, as ships imagined the enemy below. It was midnight before we subsided wearily to reflect upon our immoderate reactions to what was now evidently an utterly bemused school of whales who had enjoyed gambolling amidst pinging sound waves and whirring propellers. As for us, we had learnt the dangers of a fertile imagination in a time of high tension.

With Ascension still painting on our radars, Admiral Woodward summoned all Commanding Officers to the Flagship for his war briefing. Delivered in clipped unemotional tones, he pulled no punches. It would be tough. We could lose up to six ships before we prevailed. Our opponents had been underrated. The elements would be savage. Altogether his 'bedside manner' was less than reassuring but it was purposeful and inspiring stuff nonetheless. Our sabres were about to be used, not merely rattled after all.

On return to our ships he sent us the following signal: 'Be prepared in all respects for war by 232000Z April.' (8 pm 23rd April) Somehow I had never quite expected to see those words in print, despite having been in a fighting service for more than twenty years. Immediately, and as if to add dramatic emphasis, the weather drew in and the first of many savage gales hit us.

Over the demanding weeks that followed, my thoughts often returned to that astonishingly intense preparative interlude at Ascension and the clear-headed accuracy of that solitary face-to-face briefing. In the event, the war lasted for 45 days of bloody fighting, cost more than 1000 lives, sank four British ships and left many men scarred for life. Throughout it all our advance static 'aircraft carrier' called Ascension was hugely significant. Hercules and Nimrods from the base parachuted key stores and the lifeblood of mail to us as we ringed the Islands; airborne tankers operated round the clock to allow the RAF to reach so far south, most spectacularly giving Vulcans the 7,000 mile legs to deliver an unwelcome surprise of 10 tons of bombs onto the Stanley runway as war began; resident ship tankers acted as filling stations and providers to the 100 ships and 28,000 men that passed on their way south; and ashore the thankless and numbing task of planning and executing the colossal logistical effort was constant. The list of contributions was endless.

In charge of this frenzied activity was Captain Bob McQueen, who I remembered flying naval Sea Vixen jets with icy cool from the deck of HMS *Eagle* years earlier. A get things done Navy man, he was a scourge to all negative mentalities that arrived on 'his' Island, and much of the credit for its success could be placed at Bob's door.

And when it was all over, our gun worn out from 500 firings, ourselves weary from 30,000 miles of steaming and surviving 10 separate attacks, but with the Argentinians vanquished and the Falklands secure, where else did we stop for vital fuel and even more vital mail – but Ascension. As we limped towards our anchorage from the south, it was the words of Shakespeare's Richard II which returned to me: 'This fortress built by nature for herself . . . This precious stone set in a silver sea . . ." It had made so much possible.

Chapter 7

A View of Ascension Island from SS *Atlantic Conveyor*

by the Senior Naval Officer, Captain (later Admiral Sir) Michael Layard

To put this view in perspective it is worth reminding the reader of the evolution of *Atlantic Conveyor* in the Falklands Campaign when she was 'taken up from trade' to carry replacement aircraft, equipment and stores to the Task Force. To effect this, from concept to completion it took a little over two weeks to transform the huge container cum roll on roll off ship, laid up in Liverpool, into what could only be termed the third aircraft carrier. At Devonport Dockyard work proceeded round the clock to convert the container decks into two flight decks, fore and aft, and the accommodation altered to carry a mixed company from all the armed services, the RFA and the Merchant Navy – 127 in all, from a normal company of 25. As a result of this monumental effort, the ship was refitted, equipped, stored, manned and worked up with its Air Group of Sea Harrier, Harrier GR3, Chinook and Wessex helicopters (25 aircraft), such that we could operate as a competent unit within the Battle Group, for there, despite earlier assurances to the contrary, I had no doubt we were bound. All we lacked was any form of self-defence!

Then, after a relatively peaceful passage, in company with the *Europic Ferry*, we arrived at Ascension Island on the 4th of May 1982 to join the vast and growing Amphibious Group under the command of Commodore Michael Clapp (COMAW). Little were we to know that our next sight of the island, less than a month later, would be as 'survivors' – our great ship having been struck and sunk by Exocet missiles – and in the process we would leave twelve of our compatriots, including the redoubtable Captain Ian North, at

SS Atlantic Conveyer

the bottom of the South Atlantic. But back to the beginning and first impressions of Ascension Island were of a curious triangular island topped by greenery and cloud. The volcanic hinterland was like one imagines the surface of the moon. The island was quite clearly the focus of a multitude of activity with boats and helicopters plying a constant traffic from ship to ship and ship to shore. *Atlantic Conveyor* was something of a curiosity and visitors aplenty came to assess just what she could be capable of. The Harriers arrived from the United Kingdom and were safely recovered and stowed in their weatherproof 'overcoats' on the forward flightdeck. Meanwhile two of the Chinooks and all of the Wessex helicopters were quickly put to work transferring vast quantities of stores around the Force. In the end one Chinook was left behind to support operations on the Island. A supply of 'Sidewinder' air-to-air missiles for the Sea Harriers was delivered to the ship to give the Amphibious Force fighter defence as they made their way south to join the Battle Group. Although the Sea Harriers could only be launched vertically, thus restricting their radius of action, they would, nonetheless, be able to

The harsh volcanic landscape

The fertile top of Green Mountain

General view of the parking apron and the runway

Air defence radar on Green Mountain

Aerial view of main fuel depot

Rebuilding Wessex helicopters

A Victor refuelling another Victor

A Victor refuelling a Hercules

The Governor's residency and gardens

US Galaxy, the World's largent military transporter

The Georgetown Jetty

Airfield fuel pipeline

Hearts and Minds Project – RAF delivering banana bridge

Reverse Osmosis water plant at English Bay

counter the threat from the Argentine Boeing 707 'shadowers'. In the event, though evidently out looking for us, none came close enough!

At last, on the 7th of May all was ready and the Amphibious Group slipped quietly away, under cover of darkness, its destination the Falkland Islands 3,300 miles away. Ascension Island had played a pivotal part in preparing us for the conflict to come – an opportunity to air and discuss plans of every sort from strategic to logistic: a last chance for people, aircraft and equipment to catch up with the Task Force, and of course, the Army and Royal Marines had had a crucial leg stretch before they stepped ashore in anger. Finally, there was a huge programme of redistribution of equipment and stores. All in all, a priceless Island in a key position half way between home and conflict.

On the 18th May, *Atlantic Conveyor* began flying off Harriers to the Task Force. On 25th May, some 70 miles north-east of Port Stanley and on her way into San Carlos, she was hit port side aft by two air-launched Exocet missiles, caught fire and had to be abandoned.

Our next sight of Ascension Island was from the deck of the Esso tanker *British Tay*. She had been given the task of collecting all of the survivors from *Atlantic Conveyor* – we came from a variety of rescue ships – and to transport us, wet, nervous and travelling extremely light, to Ascension

Task force off shore

Island for onward flight home. As we stepped ashore to be warmly greeted by the Senior Naval Officer, Captain Bob McQueen and his staff, we must have looked a motley and bedraggled bunch, dressed in a variety of clothing and all carrying a brown paper bag containing our worldly possessions. An extremely efficient organisation had been set up to greet and process us. In no time, we had been issued with survivors' I.D. cards and various items of clothing. Bizarrely, we were able to buy 'duty free' as if we were returning from abroad, which we were. Then, with the prospect of a day to spend exploring the Island before flying home that night, we were whisked off in sixes and sevens by the local inhabitants, who were all marvellously kind and generous hosts. What they must have made of us I cannot imagine, for we were all a touch bruised and jumpy and quite unprepared for the warmth, understanding and comfort provided by our hosts. As evidence of this there were some emotional and tearful scenes later on as we said our farewells. For their part, I suspect, our hosts couldn't have failed to be moved by the plight and demeanour of their guests. Bob McQueen was my host and an old friend – we didn't stop talking, from start to finish, exchanging experiences and speculating on the outcome of the war and its aftermath – for if successful there would be profound political and military lessons and perceptions to emerge.

Bob took our party up Green Mountain where, in the lush greenery at the top of the volcano, we could have been in my beloved Somerset – grass, trees and even cows. Lower down, in contrast, a savage, craggy sulphurous landscape dominated by the huge airfield and surrounding supporting buildings.

The day sped by and the 'survivors' were palpably responding to the kindness of their hosts – beers in hand, smiles returning and a clear air of relaxation. My team was superbly entertained to dinner by Alan and Beth Daly. It had been a wonderfully recuperative period of adjustment before we all flew home to an emotional and joyful homecoming but tempered by grief for our lost shipmates and, in my case, disappointment that we had not been able to complete our task.

Chapter 8

THE AMPHIBIOUS TASK GROUP COMMANDER'S STORY

by Captain Michael Clapp CB, Royal Navy

It must have been during the afternoon of 3rd April, 1982, just one day after we had been alerted for operations in the South Atlantic, that Brigadier Julian Thompson and I were sitting in Hamoaze House, Plymouth, discussing the mounting of a possible amphibious operation in the Falklands. We had moved into Major General Jeremy Moore's Headquarters so that all three staffs were together. Major General Moore burst into the room to ask Julian and me where we preferred to stop on our way south, Ascension Island or St Helena. He met with rather blank expressions.

We knew roughly were the islands were. Both I knew were used by Cable and Wireless, as a school friend had spent much of his childhood on them but what else they offered I had no idea. We dived into the Admiralty Pilot book but learnt little more. Neither appeared to have much to recommend them as a place to wait; there were very few inhabitants and a good run ashore seemed most unlikely. Moreover, they were both volcanic and had steep rocky shore gradients likely to be exposed to a relentless swell, making practice landings difficult even if they had good beaches and there was little information on that score. Their anchorages were not large and were likely to be uncomfortable. Both were quite unlike the Falkland Islands and so, at first sight, of limited advantage as training areas for the troops.

The main attraction was an airfield on Ascension Island that appeared to be long enough to take large jet aircraft. But that seemed to be operated by the United States Air Force as part of their ballistic missile early warning system (BMEWS). If we could have access to that we would have a major advantage as stores and people could be flown out to join us but at about 3,500 miles from the Falklands it was unlikely to be of much help to us for offensive air operations over the Falkland Islands.

Ascension Island therefore won. We tried to find out more but beyond the fact that Napoleon had been incarcerated on St Helena and we had occupied Ascension Island with a Royal Marines contingent to deny it to any Frenchmen trying to help him escape, there simply was not much more information available to us at that time. Anyhow, we were frantically busy on a myriad of other matters and both Julian's and my staff sailed in HMS *Fearless* soon after on 6th April. It was not until we received a signal from Captain Bob McQueen on about 11th April, Easter Sunday, when about halfway to the island, that we knew what the form might be.

Bob had been flown ahead to take charge of a Naval Party to prepare the island as an advanced stores and transit base. He told us that there was only one beach at the northern end of Clarence Bay that was likely to be of any use to us and even that was subject to swell. Most of the beaches were probably too steep and were made up of soft sand which was in full use by breeding turtles which we must avoid disturbing. This caused a little light relief amongst the Royal Marines as steep sandy beaches offer dry landings and are therefore classified as 'officer's beaches' while those with shallow gradients entailing a long and wet wade they classified as 'soldiers' beaches'. Further large areas ashore were the breeding ground of the Sooty Tern and were to be out of bounds. Cats and donkeys were said to abound but little else.

At least we now knew something and our thoughts turned to training and reorganising the stow in the amphibious ships that had been so hurried – and in some cases were a cause for alarm. For instance, we found that, in the rush, petrol had been stowed below decks alongside ammunition. We badly needed to know just what was where and if possible put it in an order that allowed first day essentials to be landed first and so on.

Our first sight of the Island came on 17th April as we flew ahead to meet Admiral Fieldhouse, our Task Group Commander who had come down to brief Rear Admiral Sandy Woodward and us onboard HMS *Hermes*. The briefing was helpful and we heard we might have to wait several weeks before we were sent south to carry out a landing, if indeed the politicians found that necessary. It would be a day or two later that HMS *Fearless*, our home and headquarters, arrived at the island anchorage and we could go ashore and see for ourselves.

At the first opportunity Julian and I flew ashore to meet Bob McQueen and see what the Island had to offer. Bob had already gained a reputation for strong leadership and was having to send men back to the UK as there was no spare accommodation and they were not in his view essential. Unfortunately his view was not always shared by others, such as Julian who had asked especially for some of the people as they had a level of expertise his men lacked. Bob in other respects was clearly doing a marvellous job with very little help and we wondered what we could do to make his frantic life a little easier.

The three of us called on Bernard Pauncefort, the Resident. We hoped we reassured him that we would be as little trouble as possible but he had already realised his island would never be the same again. We also met Colonel Bill Bryden, USAF, who ran the Wideawake airport with Don Coffey the Pan Am manager who was an ex US Special Forces man. All were to be extremely helpful.

Bob appeared to be expected to visit every ship passing through but he had no boat and only a few medium support helicopters which were operating flat out on more essential tasks, so we tried to carry out that duty for him. It was convenient as several of the ships were to be part of my task group but some were to go on south to help replenish the Carrier Battle Group. We tried to help them in any way we could. We managed to visit all but one bulk fuel tanker who was unlikely to get near the war zone. She promptly complained of being disregarded!

To me the Island did not seem to offer a lot but the military were clearly pleased with what Bob and Don Coffey had to recommend. Live firing ranges were established and a shore training programme swung quickly into action. Full use was made of the Support Helicopters and Landing Craft and a massive re-stowing of stores began.

The stopover would clearly be a marvellous opportunity for me to get to know my RFA and Merchant Navy captains and for them to get to know my staff and me. It was a golden opportunity to visit their ships while at anchor and relaxed. A few RFAs had come down with me but most of the ships were joining up with *Fearless* and some escorts at the anchorage. In some ways I doubt if they were impressed by my interest. Because my Support helicopters were in frantic and important use, I tended to borrow a light helicopter or rigid raiding craft from Julian and buzzed around in an old flying suit covered with my old squadron badges. Unfortunately it soon fell apart, rotten in the tropical heat and with old age. Exploration and visiting, however, at the level my staff and I achieved could not have been done while at sea and a huge degree of confidence and trust was achieved. My arrival, for instance, soaking wet in the SS *Canberra* must have shocked their Captain in his pristine whites. On another occasion with a different ship I could only get onboard

Ships at anchor

by climbing up a rope which was rather unseemly for a Task Group Commander in some eyes, but it worked!

The opportunity to have a really good look around the ship with their Royal Navy liaison officer who I knew spoke my language was invaluable. On the *Canberra*, Captain Chris Burne gave me huge food for both pleasant and unpleasant thoughts. Pleasant because he had obviously got a good grip of the ship and the problems involved in getting her ready for war. It was marvellous to see the enthusiasm and high morale of the embarked troops. The ship was visibly shaking as many were getting fit by running around the upper deck for the umpteenth time. Others were practising weapon drills, learning advanced first aid or listening to lectures on the Falkland Islands from Major Ewen Southby-Tailyour who had commanded Naval Party 8901 in the islands a few years before. They soon learnt what to expect of the weather in which all four seasons can be expected several times a day. They heard about the treeless terrain and rock runs and, if they needed to survive on their own, to avoid Leopard Seals but eat the Tussock Grass as it was 'delicious'. Ewen's enthusiasm was boosted by the fact the *Fearless*, where he had a bunk, had run out of Port but the *Canberra* had a huge and challenging supply.

The unpleasant thoughts that arose from my visit involved the ship's appalling vulnerability to fire and battle damage, particularly it's cathedral like engine rooms. If she had to come all the way the merchant seamen would need to be properly equipped and put on war terms. What should we do to warn them and what about the ladies who were part of the crew?

My first visit to the ammunition transport *Elk* was rather more amusing. Taken up to the Master's cabin by Commander Andrew Ritchie, their liaison officer, I met Captain John Morton. He was sitting on the deck of his cabin surrounded by cases of gin and whisky. He looked hot and dishevelled with his socks rolled down. Some strange thoughts went through my mind. Happily he was quite sober and he seemed completely unfazed with his horrendous cargo. Indeed he seemed somewhat amused by all that was happening and appeared almost to relish his probable task. It was all very encouraging and I was to have the greatest admiration for the men of the Merchant Navy and RFA before the campaign was over.

High on Julian's and my priorities was the need to develop landing drills, especially from the *Canberra* and later the ferry *Norland*, both of which were likely to have to tranship troops, or even land them in the assault phase if that came to pass. *Canberra* had been fitted with two helicopter landing pads but this would be a slow method of disembarking large numbers of troops and their frontline stores. We had few enough helicopters for a force of the size the much enhanced 3rd Commando Brigade had become. If we really had to land troops from the *Canberra*, or worse rescue them, we needed to develop and practice disembarkation drills. This was achieved very successfully by using areas where gash rather than passengers was the normal occupant and every Marine and Soldier had at least one run at it.

All my merchant ships, RFAs and RN ships were put through training in damage control and, as far as possible, in air defence in inshore waters. Their hulls were checked by swimmers to make sure they made no unnecessary noise and 40 mm bofors anti-aircraft guns were flown out and fitted to the LSLs. One was purloined to provide the *Elk* with moral support as she had some 5,000 tons of mixed ammunition embarked and felt somewhat inadequately protected. Her bulwarks were also cut off and lie on the seabed off the island. This rather arbitrary operation allowed her to operate helicopters with safety and made use of her forecastle as a hangar. All helpful operationally and also very good for morale.

In a navy whose role in NATO was largely in deep waters, shore bombardment procedures were very seldom practised. The gunfire support teams were kept busy by the frigates and standards rose fast. All we lacked for training was practice in anti-aircraft defence but there was neither room at Wideawake nor at that time the ability to fly small attack aircraft out to Ascension. That was to come very soon as Harriers were fitted with in-flight refuelling probes.

One day there was a scare as a ship flying the Argentine flag had been reported snooping. It had in fact been seen a day or two before but had not been reported as it had been assumed we on *Fearless* must have seen it. It was a mistake in 'not reporting' that reminded us why Jutland had not been a resounding victory and all ships were encouraged to speak out, report and air their worries and opinions. We were concerned that a small team might have landed ashore. A search task that gave our Special Forces a little realistic fun. The risk of swimmers with limpet mines had to be considered and although little could be done by day except post armed lookouts and drop scare charges, at night the ships weighed anchor and sailed. I was hugely relieved to find no one collided but there were near misses despite a careful plan to ensure separation. It was all good training especially for the merchant ships with their Royal Naval parties embarked who were there to help communicate and explain naval operations.

The staffs of Julian's 3rd Commando Brigade and mine were still together in the *Fearless*. When not away visiting they continued their discussions and drafting written 'appreciations' which were sent back at the request of C-in-C's staff at Northwood so that a concept of operations could be created with an input from those who would have to carry it out. This meant a lot of argument and discussion but it was a useful mind-clearing exercise which had begun before we sailed from the UK. From Northwood came Major General Jeremy Moore trying hard to develop a concept of land operations which was not easy even at this stage, as there was still too little intelligence to work on. The naval concept of amphibious operations had to largely follow that of the military but decisions were reached and our recommendations were taken back to Northwood by the General.

It was an extremely busy period but one day Julian, Captain Jeremy Larken, the CO of *Fearless*, and I made time to explore a little of the island. Julian drove us in one of his Landrovers to the old Royal Marine hospital, barracks and farm near the top of Green Mountain. It was wonderfully peaceful and cool as we explored the old buildings and looked over the rest of the Island. It gave us a satisfying sense of history in some ways repeating itself and was a very welcome but short break from our worries.

Wideawake airfield was packed with aircraft and stores on every spare piece of hardstanding. I had a fascinating hour with Group Captain Jeremy

Price who had come down to help organise the RAF who were flying into Wideawake Airport in large numbers. Operation Black Buck in which one Vulcan bomber reached the Falkland Islands after numerous in-flight refuellings was happening. That it worked was a great credit to everyone involved as the aircraft had only recently been fitted with the necessary gear. The achievement of one bomb on the Stanley Airport runway was somewhat mocked but this was unfair as it is never easy to get more than one bomb on a runway when stick bombing from altitude. The main huge success of that operation was to warn the Argentines that their mainland was also in range of our bombers. They were obliged to keep aircraft deployed on the mainland that could otherwise have been thrown into the battle of the Falklands. The true effect of that raid was incalculable.

A problem arose with the large number of Press embarked on the *Canberra*. We were forbidden to let them visit the island and see the airfield. Our helicopters were in too great a demand for more essential tasks than to fly them around to visit ships. Not surprisingly they were frustrated and bored. One suspects they firmly blamed the Royal Navy and this may have been a cause for the relatively poor press received by the ships despite our efforts to send staff officers across to brief them.

To try and return some of the hospitality and help we had received we entertained onboard the key players from ashore, the ships and embarked units. Several briefings were also held by Julian's and my staffs to brief Commanding Officers and Masters on what we expected to have to do. They too were a golden opportunity to meet them on our own ground and get to know them better.

Suddenly we were ordered south in a rush. A huge amount of equipment was still ashore and our basic training programme was by no means complete. Luckily we were reprieved and managed a few more days training. However, all too soon we were ordered south. We could have used a little more time with much advantage. For instance, we had not yet managed to get the Rapier air defence missile launchers ashore and practised. They had been stowed low in the LSLs to keep them safe from the salt spray and weather but the vibration and lack of use meant they would take far too long to become fully operational in the Falklands.

In other respects our three week stay had been extremely useful. We had got to know each other better and could trust each other. We were now a team. All my ships were better known to my staff and me. They were far better prepared and the staffs now better understood the problems ahead and had made their recommendations. We now knew what was stored where. I had also been able to go ashore with Julian and witness some of the Landing Force's training, and it was clear their morale too was now high. With the exception of Rapier most drills had been practised and weapons and rifles zeroed. Everyone in the Amphibious Task Group were much better prepared for what was to come and we were at last feeling capable of going to war with some confidence. The training and re-stowing that was achieved proved vital to the subsequent success of the campaign.

None of this could have been achieved without the help of the Resident Administrator, Bernard Pauncefort, Colonel Bryden USAF and Don Coffey, but most of all that of Captain McQueen who bore the brunt of organising the frenetic merry go round that was Ascension Island. We had, I suspect, been only a small part in his hectic life but the Falklands campaign might well have turned out very differently without the help of all those in the island.

Chapter 9

THE ROYAL NAVAL REGULATORS

by Lieutenant E G Lord, Royal Navy
Naval Provost Marshal Ascension Island

———

The RN Provost Detachment on Ascension Island consisted of a Lieutenant, a Fleet Master at Arms (MAA), 2 Regulating Petty Officers (RPOs) and 3 Leading Regulators. (In the Royal Navy, the Master at Arms and the Regulating Branch are responsible for discipline.) We called ourselves, usually out of earshot of the others, 'The Magnificent Seven'. I still consider that we were most aptly named.

Three weeks after the indignation of the nation had been sorely provoked, and in my opinion, three weeks too late, it was decided to send a few Regulators to Ascension to see if any semblance of 'good order and naval discipline' could be established there. Almost overnight a dramatic change had been brought about on Ascension and this was to alter the island's way of life, probably for ever. The first naval element, mainly cooks and stores personnel had arrived with a naval captain, Captain R McQueen, RN, as the Commander British Forces Support Unit.

I was summoned to HMS *Centurion* for a briefing on Monday, April 26th, having been alerted on the preceding Friday to dig out my tropical kit, and was told by the Commodore that I would take a tried and trusted team with me to stabilise and ascertain the numbers on the island, set up a system of control and relieve the stores personnel out there and allow them to carry out the job they had been originally sent there to do i.e. the catering, stores, etc. Be ready to fly on Wednesday! You'll probably be back within the fortnight.

We gathered at RAF Lyneham, were told to change into uniform, pack everything in our bags, hand them in and were then told that we would not flying until the next morning! But what about any toilet gear, clean clothes and so on? Purely a Naval problem! One of our team had the foresight to pack a disposable razor, this was used for five different chins and the curtains and bath mats would never be the same again. This was not to be our last 'misunderstanding' with the RAF. We flew via Dakar and landed on Ascension late at night, were met and unloaded the Provost vehicle that had flown out with us on the Hercules and proceeded to find an empty tent at English Bay, one of the tented villages already established. It was pitch dark and there seemed to be a scarcity of torches and lanterns. The next morning we took over the disused and derelict Police Station in Georgetown, two rooms, one balcony and two cells, just the right type of accommodation for a team of Regulators. We scrubbed it out, chamfered it up and made it a habitable prospect. The Leading Regulators, naturally, lived in the cells and myself and the Fleet MAA shared one room, the two RPOs in the other.

Captain McQueen had promised the American authorities on Ascension Island the numbers of troops requiring food and accommodation would not exceed 200 at any one time, but when Wideawake Airfield clocked up 350 take-off and landings in one day, thus becoming for a while the busiest airfield in the world, things tended to look slightly different. My briefing from him on that first memorable morning soon made me aware of the task facing us. "Forget *Centurion* – this is what *I* want – Movements – you control them all. Accommodation – you allocate it, administer and control it. Supervision – I want an RPO in each camp (English Bay and Two Boats) as Manager – I want daily numbers on the Island broken down by service and location. I want you to do all the Regulating for Naval Party 1222 and administer discipline – and as you've brought your own transport – police coverage of all forces on the Island. Any questions?" I didn't mention it at the time, but we were half-expecting to have to deal with all the mail for the ships passing through but this task was superbly carried out by the Royal Engineers, with whom we initially shared a hut.

Also in the hut were a Squadron Leader (Admin), a Petty Officer Writer and the temporary armoury for all weapons issued to personnel on the Island. This system proved to be mutually beneficial.

Despite a few raised eyebrows from other personnel on the Island, we got on with it and an 18-hour day became commonplace for us and eventually we managed to account for all service personnel on Ascension. Prior to our arrival, details of all personnel arriving there had been written in a log and crossed through when they departed. This was obviously a potentially dangerous practice and this log had to be checked through meticulously and thoroughly without bothering the units 'down south' who had a far more important job in hand. All the movements recording had been carried out by a Colour Sergeant Royal Marines, a Petty Officer Cook and a Cook. We relieved them of this task very early. Soon a plan was devised that let us know who was expected and when, and we could consequently plan ahead. Just as things were almost getting sorted out, came the major shock of HMS *Sheffield* being sunk. We were numb and couldn't believe it – this was very close to home. In due course, *Sheffield*'s survivors passed through on their way home as did many of the others.

One amusing anecdote concerned Sheffield's personnel passing through – 2 VC10's were allocated to return them to UK. Two more Regulators arrived on the island, both Wren RPO's, to document the survivors. After a day of re-kitting, paying, issuing travel warrants, cheque books, feeding and watering and generally being regally hosted by the Islanders, the final muster was made at Wideawake and the aircraft were filled; then we thought we had one person unaccounted for. Searches were carried out and although several of the transients had imbibed rather liberally, it was considered likely that the numbers were correct and the aircraft duly left for UK.

We had all been in the vicinity, doing patrols, supervising personnel, assisting the EFI staff and acting as an information centre. When the two aircraft left, we squared up the office and concluded the business for the day; it was about 0330, and then set off back for our police station in Georgetown, some 4 miles away. About 3 miles into the journey we saw a lonely figure wandering down the side of the road. We stopped the vehicle and I alighted and approached the figure, who was dressed in Action Working Dress, and asked who he was. He identified himself from his brand new Identity Card as a member of Sheffield's company, and when we told him the flights for UK had left, he said, "I'm not worried about the skipper, I'm not particularly worried about the Jimmy (First Lieutenant), but my missus will be waiting for me at Brize Norton. Who's going to tell her?" We took him in and slept him on the balcony at the Police Station overnight and he caught the first flight back, a Hercules to Lyneham, at the next opportunity, a few hours later, clutching his duty-frees!

The accommodation problem, mainly in tents and empty houses, was eased considerably by the provision of 34 'personnel shelters' from the US authorities. These were made of compressed cardboard and were fitted complete with 12 camp beds and bedding, chairs, mop, broom and bucket! The entire complex was constructed and completed in 4 days by the US crew of 4449 MOBS. They were a thoroughly professional, competent and hard-working construction team. The accommodation was commissioned in the base at Wideawake and it was officially named 'Victory Village' but it was always known as 'Concertina City', because the units opened out like concertinas! I was told it was 'my baby', so I allowed myself the indulgence of naming the units. I named the first 26 alphabetically, in true Naval fashion, starting with Anson, Benbow, Collingwood . . . down to York and Zulu. The others we generously allowed the RAF who were to be the main occupants, to name Spitfire, Typhoon, Lancaster, etc. They obviously do not have as many famous 'names' as the Senior Service. It was a great source of entertainment to the Naval personnel to see a dozen RAF aircrew in 'Iron Duke' and 'Jellicoe' messes. Four large Portakabins were also constructed and were named Renown, Resolution, Revenge and Repulse. This went some way to 'paying back' the purely naval problem we experienced at Brize Norton!

Just prior to the 4th of July parade, which was being held in Georgetown, a diligent squadron leader based in Concertina City reported to the Provost that lady's clothing had been observed hanging out of a window in one of the accommodation units. The team were sent to investigate and found there were not illicit orgies or licentious irregularities taking place, it was merely attire for some aspiring drag-queens to participate in the parade in fancy dress.

One crime we were asked to investigate was a report of a persons or persons unknown *washing* a car in the US Base! The car was traced to a Squadron Leader and it was immediately identifiable – it was sparkling clean. He was officially warned regarding the misuse of water, a rare and precious commodity on the Island.

Numbers on the Island tended to stabilise and remained fairly static after the initial push south and was usually about 800 RAF personnel, 80 RN and about 100 Army from all regiments. We were assisted tremendously by the US authorities who fed most of us who were accommodated in the Georgetown/Wideawake areas, provided some accommodation and some recreational facilities.

A very moving memorial service took place in the tiny Georgetown church one Sunday. It was a seafarer's service for the fallen in the Falklands. A tanker arrived just in time for the Captain of the *Atlantic Conveyor*'s naval party and other survivors to be helicoptered in, still battle weary and showing signs of wear. 'Eternal Father strong to save' has seldom had such significance. The church service was followed by a march past of all the island's Brownies, Guides, Scouts and Cubs and the salute was taken by Captain McQueen, just outside the Provost Headquarters. We made a point of flying the largest possible White Ensign at all times and we had acquired one of the largest available from the *Fearless*, when she passed through on her way south. To pay for this 'rabbit' we had provided a ceremonial sunset party when Fearless entertained the local community with a 'beat retreat' on the Parade Ground.

Discipline was reasonably easy to maintain, as most people were either too busy or too tired to indulge in that great catalyst, booze, but one or two isolated incidents were dealt with swiftly and smoothly. One involved a RAF airman, who was reported to be drunk at the Governor's Residency way up on Green Mountain. We collected the miscreant, arrested him and transported him back to his unit. He was tried summarily, received a substantial fine and the Leading Regulators attended his trial and impressed several senior RAF officers with their professionalism, tact and versatility.

Probably my proudest memory was when the Falklands Campaign was all over bar the shouting. We had first met Colonel Chaundler when he flew out via Ascension Island to take the place of Colonel H Jones VC who had been killed in the Falklands. When the Paras, there were 1,068 of them, returned to Ascension Island to be flown home to the UK, Colonel Chaundler, led his men from the jetty to the airfield. My MAA and myself stood by the side of the road as he was leading them in to the airfield where aircraft were waiting to return them to UK. We saluted and requested permission to march with the Paras. He responded and said "You're most welcome, this was the Navy's war and we wouldn't be here today without the efforts of your lads – March up front with me". We marched either side of him and considered it to be a great honour.

To celebrate the birth of Prince William, we organised a 'splice the mainbrace' purely for the naval personnel of NP1222. One resourceful Leading Regulator made a rum tub and decorated it properly and the full ceremony was held at the Provost Headquarters, when all entitled personnel had their 'tot' in the time honoured fashion.

When the sad day came for Captain McQueen to leave Ascension to return home, we made sure his departure would not go unnoticed. I detailed two Leading Regulators to 'pipe the side' as he went up the aircraft steps and when he reached the top the Fleet MAA and myself unfurled a very large and very clean White Ensign as a backdrop. His final words were before he left Ascension were, "Trust the Regulators to get it right". That, for me, succinctly summed up our efforts and made us fully aware of how much we had been appreciated.

Eventually, after three most enlightening months, the Magnificent Seven were relieved by 18 RAF personnel (to allocate accommodation) and 5 Royal

Corps of Transport (the latter purely for movements) when everyone else was going home. It seemed to me that they'd missed the main show.

With hindsight, the time we spent on Ascension Island was extremely busy, we practised everything we'd been trained to do, learned a great deal and a whole lot more beside.

The RN Regulators at Ascension Island were:

Lieutenant (X) (Reg) E G Lord
Fleet Master-at-Arms D J Mounce
Regulating Petty Officer R L Payne (promoted whilst at ASI)
Regulating Petty Officer T Wright
Leading Regulator E J Beaton
Leading Regulator W A Ferguson
Leading Regulator I Rigby.

Chapter 10

ARGENTINE PRISONERS OF WAR

———

On 25th April, the battle for South Georgia had been won and on 2nd May HMS *Antrim* and RFA *Tidespring* set sail for Ascension Island. On board HMS *Antrim* under guard in Captain Young's day cabin was Lieutenant Commander Alfredo Ignacio Astiz, who had commanded the Argentinian marine garrison on South Georgia, of whom more later. RFA *Tidespring* carried 151 prisoners of war, 39 Argentinian civilian scrap workers, two British Antartic Survey teams, two lady ornithologists (Miss Annie Price and Miss Cindy Buxton) and their two pet ducks!

By the 11th June, *Tidespring* was 240 miles from Ascension, and we launched a Chinook with the International Committee of the Red Cross (ICRC) team to inspect the conditions under which the prisoners were being held. This team was headed by M André Tschiffeli and the two other members were Dr Michel Hubert and M Jean Pierre Givel. We also sent a Special Investigation Branch team who were allowed by the Red Cross to interview the prisoners under the Geneva Convention rules. Throughout my dealings with the Red Cross, I was most impressed by their tact, charm and professional attitude to their unusual task. They reported that, 'under the circumstances', the conditions under which the prisoners were being held were satisfactory.

Our task was to transfer the 190 Argentinians from *Tidespring* and *Antrim* to a chartered Dutch Martinair DC10 for onward journey to the Argentine. We decided to do this after dark so that they would see as little of our arrangements as possible. Three helicopters, two Wessex 5s and a Sea King Mk3 brought them ashore and air-conditioned buses with blacked out windows were used to carry them from the helicopters to the DC10. They were a motley crew, many seasoned and tough-looking, perhaps special forces trained and the other group young national servicemen. One young man came up to me and asked, "Excuse me , Sir, I am due to go up to Oxford in October. Do you think they'll still have me?" I confessed not to know the answer but wished him luck.

We had also decided that we would load all the others before bringing Lieutenant Commander Astiz ashore. Perhaps this was just as well because a few minutes before this was due to happen, the red secure phone rang, summoning me to talk. "You are not to return Astiz to the Argentine on this plane" a voice said. I explained that I should have to inform the Red Cross. André Tschifelli was sanguine – "I thought that it was all going too smoothly. But I shall have to register a protest because he was declared on the repatriation list." I explained this on the red phone, to receive the reply that there was a lady standing beside the person at the other end and that I had better get on with implementing what she had decided! I did just that!

Some background may be helpful. During the 'dirty war', Lieutenant Commander Alfredo Astiz had been in the Naval Mechanical School in Buenos Aires and was convicted *in absentia* by a French court of the murder of two nuns, Sisters Alice Doman and Sister Renée-Leonie Duquet. The Swedish government were also interested in the death of a Swedish-Argentine teenage girl. This was why Mrs Thatcher, for it was indeed she, wanted to look further into whether he could be brought to justice for these crimes.

I called the most senior Argentinian officer, Lieutenant Commander Bicain, out of the DC10 and explained that Lieutenant Commander Astiz would not be coming with them. He attempted to give me an argument, was overruled and returned to his seat in the aircraft. Further protestations among the other Argentinians were diffused by a very attractive Dutch air hostess walking down the cabin with a tray of drinks, doors were closed and the aircraft took off at 0200.

I then flew out to HMS *Antelope*, the ship to which Lieutenant Commander Astiz had been transferred, to inform him that he would be kept at Ascension and returned to the UK in due course. He was transferred to HMS *Dumbarton Castle* the next day, where he was placed under the guard of Lieutenant Mills, Royal Marines and the *Endurance* detachment of Royal Marines who had been his captives on South Georgia.

I decided that it would be more secure to keep this high risk prisoner offshore and, of course, the Marine guard had a special interest in making sure that he did not attempt to escape.

It speaks volumes for the ICRC that André Tshifelli returned to Ascension on the 24th May to visit Astiz and his accommodation in the *Dumbarton Castle* and to view his accommodation in the *British Avon*, the ship in which he returned to UK.

I visited Astiz twice, once by myself and the second time with André. He struck me as a most intelligent but ruthless young officer. He spoke fluent English with an upper class accent. He had no complaints about his conditions.

On return to the UK, he was detained for a period in Colchester Military Prison while the Attorney General investigated the possibility of bringing him to justice and the legality of handing him over to either the French or the Swedish. Under the Geneva Convention it is not permissible to prosecute someone for actions in previous wars, so he was returned to the Argentine and subsequently benefited from a law passed in 1986 which limited prosecutions. He retired from the Argentine Navy in 1996 as a Captain.

Chapter 11

AN AMERICAN TALE

by William D Bryden, Lt Col USAF, Ret.

———

I first saw Ascension Island while on a communications test mission flying in the South Atlantic and Indian Oceans. I was intrigued by its stark beauty and isolation from the rest of the world. One day in early 1981, I met by chance with the Commander of the US Air Force Eastern Test Range and asked him in passing when they were going to make the assignment as Ascension US Base Commander an accompanied tour (it had always been a one year unaccompanied tour of duty). He replied, "We just did, are you interested?" "Let me talk it over with my wife and I will let you know tomorrow", was my reply. From that offhand comment Mary Lou and I ended up travelling to Ascension Auxiliary Air Field for a two-year tour of duty starting in June of 1981. Our two sons were both in college so this was an ideal time in our lives to take on such an isolated tour.

Our first nine months were filled with getting to know the island and its people.

The US mission there was to track and gather data from the many various satellites traveling overhead and many of the missiles flown down the Eastern Test Range. We leased our base from the United Kingdom and operated the airfield primarily to fly in our people and supplies. The airfield has a rich history surrounding its role in WWII. Our agreement called for the US to provide logistic support to the UK Forces should they require it. This would become rather important sooner than I could have imagined.

The airfield, known as Wideawake Airfield because of the Wideawake terns that nest alongside the field, was built in 1942 in less than six months.

It was originally six thousand feet long and was extended to ten thousand feet in the early 1960s in support of NASA joining the Eastern Test Range in using the base for communications and data gathering. We typically had two or three scheduled flights per week with a handful of other arrivals supporting various military missions, both UK and US. The British civilian companies on the island had five charter flights per year to support moving their folks on and off the island. Our average monthly aircraft arrivals for the year prior to the Falklands War was 24.4. Things were going to change!

April 2nd, 1982 – a call from a London newspaper

On the morning of April 2nd, 1982, I received a phone call from a reporter claiming to represent one of the London newspapers. He wanted to know how many aircraft were on their way to Ascension from the UK, and how far was it from our base to the Falkland Islands. I had no idea what had prompted the questions, I knew of no aircraft on their way to us, and I told the person that if he would hold for a moment I would check on the distance to the Falklands. I had a large wall map of the Atlantic Ocean and adjacent land areas. I estimated the distance (I am a Navigator by training) and passed on the information.

As it turns out, we were situated very close to half way between the UK and the Falklands, a most fortunate position for what was to come. That phone call was my notification of the start of the war in the Falklands. Fortunately, later in that day we had a previously planned meeting of the heads of the Island organizations. By that time each of us had received additional information concerning what was going on. However, as much as we guessed what was to come we seriously underestimated what was going to be asked of this tiny island.

Can we take 5 C-130 Hercules over the next 3 days?

The first official request I received for support was a telegram asking if we could take five C-130 Hercules aircraft over the next three days. They would be arriving with supplies for ships which were on their way and would stop at Ascension to be re-supplied. We would need to unload the aircraft, refuel them, provide crew quarters and feed the crews before their departure after twelve or so hours on the ground. We had one barracks with about 15 empty rooms which we used for aircrew quarters and we had our regular aircraft due in three days but we thought we could find a way to manage. Well, that was just the start, we had five aircraft in before the end of the second day and the traffic kept increasing. Several days later our Base Manager, Don Coffey (Pan American provided all our base management and maintenance functions under contract to the USAF), called me to come have a look at our dining hall.

Without question, Brian Joshua, our dining hall manager, put on the finest spread on the Island. Our dining hall routinely fed the 450 people who lived and worked on the US Base. On this day, for the noon meal, almost every visiting troop had found his way to the dining hall. The line which was seldom longer than ten or fifteen people now wound out the doors and several hundred feet down the street. Our guys were cooking as fast as they could. By the end of the meal they had served over 900 meals, more than double the normal.

Airfield and base operations – before and after
By the second week we were supporting over a hundred extra people on our base and the airfield operations were now running close to 24 hours a day. The demand on the dining hall required an extra C-141 from Patrick AFB (our home base) because we were running through food at twice the normal rate. This was true of other organizations on the Island also.

Water supplies grow short
Ascension has no supply of fresh water. All drinking water on Ascension is made by removing the salt from seawater, which we had plenty of! Both the US Base and the BBC power station made water for the Island. The base used the heat from our generating station to distill fresh drinking water. Just prior to the start of hostilities we had taken our system down for routine overhaul. We had full tanks but they were rapidly being used up and our folks were having problems getting the system back in operation. We called for a back-up reverse osmosis system but were initially refused. I must admit I was upset by the decision and suggested they fill a glass with salt water and set it in front of the General who was making the decision. Then remind him that this is what we would be drinking in less than four days. We got down to less than two days supply, but the RO unit finally showed up. Fortunately both it and our main system were in operation by the next day. It took the next two weeks to get our tanks refilled.

Concertina City appears
We made every empty barracks room available and still needed more. Within two weeks we had numerous aircraft stationed at our base. We now

had several helicopters here to resupply the passing ships, and well over 500 troops permanently stationed on the Island. The US Army Rapid Deployment Force was called on to provide some relief. They arrived with their equipment on several C-141 aircraft. Each aircraft pallet held several folded up huts. When they were opened up each one would house ten people in air-conditioned comfort. They came complete with beds, tables, and chairs. They also set up washroom facilities, a dining space, and a generating facility that provided power for the camp. Because of the way the units unfolded they resembled concertinas, and the area became known as Concertina City.

Aviation fuel shortage – a fuel line is constructed

As with most other things on Ascension, our fuel supplies were designed to meet our normal needs and a one-time emergency. Well, this emergency was going well beyond what could be called 'one time'. We were fortunate to have had a fuel ship in our harbor when the hostilities started. They were going to top up our storage tanks and leave within a few days, going to their next port of call. Within several days we were using aviation fuel many times faster than normal and it was now obvious that things were going to get worse

Setting up Concertina City

before they got better. With a few phone calls to some logically thinking people we were able to have the tanker stay in our harbour and deliver all its fuel to our tanks. Several weeks later, when the tanker ran low, the British had a BP tanker (the *British Esk*) come in and stay in harbour supplying fuel for the remainder of the big push. That took care of getting fuel into our tanks on shore. But these tanks were several miles from the airfield. We now had many road tankers going back and forth at a great rate. The British Forces came to the rescue. Within less than two weeks they engineered, flew in, assembled, and had in operation, a pipeline running the full distance from the tank farm to the airfield. They installed several large rubber bladders at the airfield to hold fuel there for delivery to the aircraft. We did have a leak or two, but all were fixed quickly and the system saved a great amount of wear and tear on our trucks and the roads.

The UK forces get organized
For the first several days, crews were staying only for a short time, unloading their cargo and then going on their way. By the end of the first week some people were sent down to sort and manage the arrival and departure of cargo. The next step up was the arrival of several helicopters

The fuel pipe line

to provide the means to get supplies quickly to the ships. As the numbers continued to grow it became obvious that some unity of command on Ascension was required. This went through several phases but with the arrival of Captain Robert McQueen, RN, we had a command structure that made everyone's job easier. It is always easier when you have one source for answers and direction.

A division of duties – UK run the military operations

With a unified command structure in place I could now stay on top of what was coming by working with Capt McQueen and his staff, and be confident that I had the true picture of what we should be prepared to support. I mentioned earlier that we had in place, before all this started, an agreement calling for the US to provide logistical support should the UK Forces require it. I don't believe anyone foresaw this level of support, but the agreement provided a basis for the effort being expended.

US run airfield operations and safety

While in no way uncomplicated, our relationship with the British forces was comfortable. They were responsible for the running of their war; we were responsible for the safe and efficient operation of the airfield and the supporting elements on the American base at Ascension. We had the advantage of being able to view the airfield operations as a disinterested party, notifying our new users when their operations strained the bounds of safety and common sense. Some examples follow.

Bombs and missiles need a home

One morning, several weeks into the operation, I was touring the parking ramp. (Wideawake Field had one parking area located to the right side of the single runway as viewed from a normal approach. I should also mention no taxiways, just a runway and a parking area.) I noticed a cluster of three 500 pound bombs stacked at the edge of the paved area, just behind a RAF Nimrod. Munitions are normally loaded on an aircraft immediately before its mission or stored in a weapons storage facility. Ascension did not have such a facility. We had never had need of such an area.

I grabbed Don Coffey, my Base Manager, and off we went to 'discuss' the matter with Capt McQueen and Group Captain Jeremy Price, his senior RAF staff officer. My first question, "Is this common practice at an RAF Base?"

"No! What can we do?"

"Build a storage area"

"How long will it take?"

This is where Don jumped in and said that, if the RAF could get us a section of culvert to allow a road to bridge a drainage area he could construct a bunkered earthen storage area within three days. They did and we did. All future weapons were stored safely well away from the aircraft and well off our airfield.

Victors arrive – with drag chutes!

We were asked if we could find room on our parking area for several RAF Victor tanker aircraft. They were needed to refuel some of the other aircraft operating out of Ascension now that we were several weeks into the war. I made my way up to our control tower to watch their arrival. It is always interesting to watch first time landings at Ascension. The runway rises for the first two thousand feet, and then it drops away rather quickly for the next five thousand feet. The effect is such that if you don't get your wheels down in the initial part of the runway you can end up chasing the runway as it falls away from you. Our tower operators would always warn new arrivals of these conditions, but it was still fun to watch the reactions.

On this day the surprise was on us. The first Victor touched down about a thousand feet in from the approach and began his rollout. Then to our surprise he deployed a drag chute! No one told us that this was standard procedure for the Victors. Evidently their standard practice was to use the drag chute until they reached a reasonable speed then drop it on the runway for some ground crew to pick up.

With three other Victors in the pattern, and the only runway blocked with a parachute we had to scramble to get a crew of our ground handlers to get in their pickups and get out on the runway and retrieve the chute. They look light but with their size they are quite heavy. It was all that two guys could do to get the chute in the back of their truck. Once cleared the Victor was then able to taxi back up the runway and into the parking ramp. Now the second Victor could land. We developed a new procedure on the spot! From now on the Victors would not release their chutes until they had taxied back up the runway and had turned onto the parking ramp. This still required each Victor to taxi back and clear the runway before the next could land. Slow but workable under normal conditions. And one more unexpected event dealt with.

Sidewinders arrive at 2 am

The US had sold the British a large number of Sidewinder missiles and was to deliver them by C-141. Well, they arrived on our airfield at 2 am! I was called out of bed to take possession of them. We unloaded the aircraft and I counted the missiles, then I signed for many millions of dollars worth of hardware. I was very relieved the next morning when I was able to get the UK munitions people to take them off my hands and sign for them.

Harriers burn up our only runway

The Harrier aircraft are an interesting mix of airplane and blowtorch. They first arrived en route to *Atlantic Conveyor*. Later we had three assigned to Ascension to provide protection should the Argentines decide to try and cut the supply lines at this point. The Harrier has always wowed the spectators with its vertical takeoffs and landings. These usually take place on surfaces prepared for their jet blast. Our runway was asphalt and could not stand up to prolonged jet engine thrust. After the first Harrier vertical takeoff we were able to demonstrate this to our UK visitors. We had a burn in the center of the runway, about one thousand feet in from the approach end, which was about twenty feet wide, forty-five feet long and over eight inches deep in the center. We got some quick patching material flown in the next day and had it repaired in less than three days. In the mean time all aircraft were restricted from the first part of the runway. Oh yes, another new directive. No vertical take-offs or landings for the Harriers at Ascension!

And then the runway lights go out

Before the war we had used our runway at night no more than two or three times a week, and then for no more than twenty or thirty minutes at a time. Once the Falklands support was under way we had the runway lit for many hours every night. One night it happened. The lights on the last third of the runway failed. Within hours the remaining lights failed. We had several planes inbound so we put our back up programme in action. The flight line crew went to the supply store and checked out every road flare pot we had in stock. (These were those small round pots, filled with kerosene and a lighted wick to warn people of dangers along the roads.) They were spaced down both sides of the runway and we planned to light them when the aircraft was a few minutes from landing. Fortunately the crews tried to light a few of them and found it took quite a bit of effort to get them going. Another great idea came to the rescue. The guys borrowed an acetylene torch, and then sat with it in the back of a flight line pick up truck. One of the flight line crew would drive down the runway, pausing briefly at each pot while the guy in the back would hit the wick with the torch. It worked. They were able to light all the pots in about ten minutes.

That would be the end of the story if it hadn't been for the departure of a C-5 Galaxy. As it rolled down the runway, after picking up some speed, the vortex off of each wingtip put out each pot as it rolled past. These flare pots were obviously a short time fix. The RAF flew in a portable runway lighting system about two days later. It took about six hours to install. This system worked very well and provided light for about a month while the main system was repaired. This is just one more example of how each of us, UK and US, were working together to make do! No one ever said, 'We fixed the last problem; it's your turn!' We would look for solutions and took pride in getting the job done, no matter who came up with the plan or who carried it out.

'Help' from the Pentagon

A short time into the war I was told I was to get some 'help' from the Pentagon, in the form of a Major from the Defense Intelligence Agency. After several protestations – no room, limited food and water, no time for orientation, etc. – it became clear that this was not a request, it was an order. So several days later my new Assistant Base Commander (his cover story) arrived. I took Major Dan Webster with me on a day's travel and introduced him to the island leadership. Over a drink at the Exiles Club that evening Bernard Pauncefort, the Island Administrator, asked me who the 'spook' was. I could see that our cover story didn't fool anyone.

A day or two later Dan asked me to take him out to a point where he could observe the shipping in our harbour. There was an ideal location next to one of our radar telemetry sites and I delivered him there. He went equipped with field glasses, a large tablet, and a copy of *Jane's Fighting Ships*. I left him to his task and told him to call when he needed a ride back to the base. Shortly before my daily call to my home base, Patrick AFB in Florida, I picked him up and we went to make our daily report.

I started with my usual rundown of base status, food, water, fuel supply, immediate needs, projected needs, and so forth. Then I ran down the daily arrivals and departures of all the aircraft and ships at Ascension and finished up with a rundown of all the aircraft on the airfield and all the ships in the harbour. I noticed that as I ran down the list of ships in the harbour that Dan was looking down at his notes from the day with astonishment. When I finished he asked me where I had gotten the list of ships. It matched the list he had spent the day compiling, ship for ship. "I go out to the British Forces headquarters each day and copy the list of ships from their grease-board." I replied, so much easier than spending the day trying to identify them through field glasses!

Major Webster spent about two weeks with us before he was able to convince his masters that all the activities on Ascension were being properly reported and that our British visitors were being very open about all their operations on our base. I believe he was glad to leave and we were glad to get the extra bed space back.

Night of the Vulcan raid on Port Stanley

Almost by accident, I sat in on a briefing of the plans to get a Vulcan bomber from Ascension to Port Stanley to attempt to bomb the runway there. Let me describe a few activities that accompanied the main mission of that first night raid.

First off, a bombing raid from our airfield fell outside of what I considered 'logistical support'. I gave Capt McQueen a letter saying that Ascension AAF should not be used as the point of departure for such a raid, and then sent off a quick message to my Headquarters requesting instructions.

Within four hours I was told to provide whatever support the British Forces requested. Directions like that were easy to follow – the raid was on.

Four Victors return at one time – all low on fuel

On the night of the raid, numerous Victor tankers took off at various times to place themselves at the proper refuelling locations along the route to Port Stanley. As a result, four Victors (remember, the planes with the drag chutes) arrived back at Ascension, after topping off the Vulcan bomber and other Victors heading South, very low on fuel and all needing to get down on their first approach.

We quickly calculated that there wasn't time to have them land and taxi back off the runway one at a time. The run out end of the runway did have a wide turnaround pad. Working with the RAF duty officer who was with us in the control tower, we quickly decided that each aircraft should land, retain its drag chute, and taxi to the turnaround pad. The first to pull as far left as possible, the second as far right as possible, and the third straight ahead. This blocked the end of the runway so we instructed the fourth aircraft to plan on departing the runway to the left (a volcanic cinder field) should he not be able to stop within normal distances. This would save the airfield and the other three aircraft. Fortunately our plan for the fourth aircraft wasn't needed; all landed safely. After we all breathed a few deep breaths our ground crews picked up the four drag chutes and the four Victors cleared the runway.

This was just one of many brave and harrowing feats of the 1st May raid. This effort to carry out a raid on a target over 3300 miles away had many dangerous elements. That it succeeded is a testament to the great planning and outstanding flying by all involved.

A long night as we count them back safely
The Vulcan bomber dropped its 21 1,000 pound bombs at 4:46 am Port Stanley time (7:46 am Ascension time), over eight hours after its departure from Ascension. In all, over twenty aircraft were involved in getting the single Vulcan to its destination and we waited with great anticipation for each and every one of them to return safely to Ascension. It was early afternoon by the time all the aircraft had returned safely. In the tower we recorded each departure and marked each one back as it touched down safely. This was a long and successful night and day.

A remarkable record
Training is a great help in a time of conflict. The men and women of Ascension Auxiliary Airfield had no warning that they were going to be called on to provide the level of support required by the British forces in April through June of 1982, but they were ready to do their job and do it well, because each of them had been trained for their task over many years. To give you some idea of the size of this operation I will give a few before and after numbers concerning the operations on Ascension AAF.

Flight operations numbers (Aircraft arrivals at Ascension AAF)
For the 12 months prior to April 1982 – 24.4 aircraft per month
For April, 1982 (The start of hostilities) – 3607 aircraft
This included 13 US aircraft, 1 British civilian, all others MOD
For May, 1982 – 2082 aircraft
For June, 1982 – 1800 aircraft

The busiest week (23rd to 29th April) had 1573 arrivals. That averages to over 224 arrivals per day. While this is no record for airport operations this is incredibly busy for an airport with a single runway and no taxiways.

MOD Aircraft Arrivals – April 1982 through March 1983

RAF C-130 Hercules – 1512
RAF VC-10s – 460
RAF Nimrods – 279
RAF Victors – 1437
RAF Vulcans – 19
RAF/RN Harriers – 74
RAF F-4 Phantoms – 478
RAF Buccaneers – 6
Civil Belfast freighters – 50
Civil Other Charters – 6
RAF/RN Helicopters – 12,603
TOTAL MOD – 16,924

Flight safety record

Without question, we were finding ways to get the job done, but not without an eye to safety. We did cut corners from time to time, but always with a calculated effort to maintain safe practices. We did land a Victor with three other Victors still on the runway, but it was the safest action to take, rather than risk an aircraft running out of fuel while waiting to land. We did conduct night operations with flare pots for runway lighting, but the nearest airfield to Ascension is over 911 nautical miles away! Not a good alternative!

The only reportable incident during the April 1982 to March 1983 period involved an F-4 tail section that was on its shipping dolly, sitting in the parking area. Its brakes were not properly set and it was caught by the prop blast of a taxiing C-130 and blown across the ramp where it hit the side of a USAF C-135. It caused a tear in the skin of the fuselage and required sheet metal repair.

Were we lucky? Yes! But good training, and good procedures had a major hand in our safe operation.

The dedicated people – St Helena airfield ground operations crews

For many years PanAm had hired and trained men from St Helena to staff our base security force. Their additional duty was to support arriving and departing aircraft. This involved marshalling arriving and departing aircraft, loading and unloading cargo, and refuelling each aircraft. At two to three aircraft a week this was a reasonable additional duty. When the UK Forces arrived in April of 1982 this became a 24-hour a day job. The security group was divided into two units and they worked 12 hours on, 12 off, seven days a week, for over six weeks, until additional people could be hired and trained. To their immense credit I never once heard a complaint. They did their job, and did it well!

Tower operators (ATC) in short supply
At the start we had two tower operators with additional duties on our base. They worked twelve hours on, twelve hours off for close to two months supporting the greatly increased airfield operations. Finally, toward the middle of May we were able to get several additional tower controllers in place and checked out but without the dedication of our original controllers the success and safety of this action would have suffered.

US Base people work hard to provide support
Not so obvious was the job being done by many other people on our base. The cooks and dining hall staff were feeding more than twice the numbers they had just a few weeks before, and with no additional staff. Our fuel farm staff was handling close to ten times the fuel of just three weeks before. And our people that ran the club and movie theatre found their number of patrons increase dramatically. This was true throughout the island, not just on our base. While there were no commercial enterprises on Ascension, the people of the Island opened their clubs and their homes to the forces stationed on Ascension as well as those that were passing through.

Recognition
Prime Minister Thatcher, on her way back from a visit to the Falklands shortly after the end of hostilities, spent an hour with the people of Ascension. Her thanks for our support were generous and appreciated.

To a greater extent the many plaques I received from the various units that we supported at our airfield still make me feel proud of our contribution. They hang on the wall in my den as a constant reminder of a very busy time in the life of Ascension Auxiliary Air Field.

This was a strange time on a most unusual Island. I wish war on no one, but I am glad I was on Ascension at this time and hope that our base and its people contributed to the quick end of hostilities.

Chapter 12

A Civilian's Tale

by Norman Shacklady BBC Resident Engineer

———

Before the Falklands War, being a resident of Ascension Island meant living on a relatively little known volcanic outcrop, along with a mere handful of other people, and being very much aware of just how remote we all were from the rest of the world. Our main connection with the UK was a chartered aircraft which made five trips a year. When a charter flight left for its return to the UK, many of us would gather on the adjacent 'Command Hill' to watch its departure. It's difficult to express one's feelings as the aircraft slowly disappeared, leaving behind just the sound of the wind and the sight of an empty airstrip; it was always a poignant moment. In an emergency one could return home on an American military flight to Antigua and thence onwards, an uncomfortable, expensive and often lengthy process. Not being on any of the shipping lanes, the South Atlantic presented a wide vista of emptiness, broken only occasionally by a passing yacht calling in to pick up supplies. Not you may say, an idyllic picture; however, there were many compensations for making home among the 42 volcanoes which make up this unique island, and for most people, leaving it was nearly always a sad occasion. Suddenly though in April 1982 all this was to change, and eventually we were to find ourselves in the centre of an incredible amount of activity, noise and many strangers. Not only that, our island was suddenly headline news, and relatives at home reading 'too much between the lines', worried for our safety.

It all began fairly slowly with the arrival of several RAF Hercules aircraft on Sunday 4th of April, bringing in a group of servicemen who had to be

The only telephone line to the MOD

found accommodation and messing. As the military had no facilities on the island, apart from two empty Nissen huts used occasionally by the RAF on exercise, this was the first problem; in fact a problem which was to remain throughout the conflict. Such resources that did exist were those of the resident organisations, and then only sufficient to support their own particular needs. Two Boats village, where my wife and I lived, consists of prefabricated bungalows, and there were a number of spares for use when staff changed over at charter time. As the number of service personnel increased these were given over to the military, but they could only accommodate a small number of men. However, in true service style these were made good use of, and stories of three piece suites and refrigerators moving mysteriously through the village in the dead of night were not uncommon. When they were eventually handed back to us we scrapped the original inventories and started again!

Shortly after all this began, I received a telephone call from a London based newspaper correspondent who had made his way to Antigua. We were having an Italian Night at the BBC's 'Klinka Klub' when the call was put through to me. I should explain that at that time on Ascension we had a manual telephone exchange operated by Cable and Wireless. It was one of those rather nice civilised touches that if you were not at home the operator would ring round to the most likely places to find you. This chap, unable to get any further under his own steam, and having been given my name, asked if I could as a matter of urgency organise a flight for him and book him into a decent hotel! Such was the level of ignorance about Ascension, even amongst the press.

As the weeks passed the number of servicemen arriving continued to grow, and every possible kind of accommodation was employed to house them. Anything with a roof was fair game, even some garages in the village became 'desirable residences'. Soon the demand far outstripped the availability and new arrivals were often sent out to find somewhere for themselves. I recall a burly Chief Petty Officer in charge of a small party turning up one morning at my office, asking if I had anything to offer, ". . . any old hut will do sir, we'll be no trouble, we can look after ourselves". It all needed a certain amount of initiative. I remember an old disused club premises in the village being put to good use as a cookhouse and mess hall. Eventually tented areas appeared and some men were housed in the American sector; they were probably the lucky ones.

One tented unit was situated near to English Bay close to my own organisation the BBC, and at that time we were having difficulty in raising a committee to run our 'Klinka Klub', also nearby. These poor chaps had a problem, with little or no transport they were miles from the nearest clubs in Georgetown and Two Boats where in the evening they could have a beer and relax. We had a brilliant idea. Why not under certain agreed conditions, give them the option to run the club and we could all benefit. They became the envy of many other units, not only did they have full access to a club on their doorstep, they even ran it themselves. I have to report that it ran with military precision, and we had not the slightest problem during the whole time they were there.

By now the task force had arrived and our empty ocean suddenly became awash with shipping and a scene of hectic activity. Helicopters carrying stores that had arrived on the island by air made constant sorties to and from the waiting ships. Amongst the many ships at anchor was the familiar sight of the *Canberra*, which was being used as a troop ship, and earlier, in stark contrast, the impressive aircraft carrier HMS *Hermes*. On board *Hermes* were a number of news correspondents, one of which was the BBC's Brian Hanrahan. Knowing that there was a 'BBC man' on the island, he sent me an invitation to meet him and have dinner on the ship, but regretfully the MOD people on the island refused to allow the visit. At the time there was a news black-out as to what was going on, and clearly they thought that Hanrahan might use the occasion to file a report back to London. It raised

The canteen set up by locals for troops in transit

the thought that I might not be considered trustworthy; something that as a head of an organisation on the island I resented deeply.

To relieve the inevitable boredom of being cooped up on *Canberra*, troops were sent ashore each day, not that there was much for them to do, but it must have been a welcome relief for them. Apart from the American sector, there were only two shops that supplied our daily needs, one in Georgetown and the other in Two Boats. It so happened that they were uniquely supplied and operated by NAAFI and had been so for some years, they were both quite small and they just about kept pace with our demands – most of the time anyway. To the troops the fact that they were NAAFI shops meant that they could use them, and it was very difficult to convince them that this was not the case. There were no other shops so one can appreciate both their frustration and our concern. With precious little to occupy them, the vicar's wife organised the setting up of a canteen on the patio of the Saints Club in Georgetown. This much needed facility was run by the UK and St Helenian wives and proved to be a huge success, not only with the troops but also with those running it who felt that they were contributing to the general effort. I recall an episode when one of the residents of Georgetown and some friends were gathered on his patio having a few drinks. A lone serviceman appeared, who by all accounts had had a few anyway, sat at an empty table and to everyone's surprise ordered a beer. I suspect that he probably returned to his ship thinking that some of the bars on the island were very friendly places! It is only a short journey to the American Base, and there they were welcome to use the Base Exchange (lots of goodies) and a small gift shop which was set up and managed by the Base Commander's wife. Their Volcano Club and snack bar was a popular watering hole, not just for the troops, but we civilians also.

The sight of servicemen in battledress carrying arms and the skies full of military aircraft became quite normal. I can recall young St Helenian children in particular looking on in obvious amazement, having never before witnessed such things, many would not have even seen videos; at that time there were very few VCR's on the island. This effect on the children was highlighted when the usual annual children's competition was held to design a poster for the Ascension Day Fair, which raises money for the local church. Without exception every entry depicted the church being furiously attacked by aircraft dropping bombs and soldiers firing all manner of guns. I can't remember how we solved that one!

All my expatriate staff were transmission engineers apart from one, my Administration Officer. He was a studio man whose base was Bush House in London, and along with his administration duties he was required to send back to London any material which Bush House might find useful for World Service programmes. This generally meant interviewing people of interest who might be passing through, such as round the world yachtsmen or specialists en-route to and from St. Helena. Now he found himself sitting on top of the biggest story he would ever likely come across in his entire career, and was unable to file a single line back to London. The poor chap found it hard going, but nevertheless managed to retain his sanity before eventually returning to the U.K. Early in the proceedings, it had been made abundantly clear to me by the Administrator that we were to remain silent, regardless of what we witnessed or heard; I think there was some mention of being locked in a certain 'Tower' if we transgressed!

We became aware that the wild donkeys which roam the island had suddenly disappeared, and various attempts to locate them failed to make any sightings. Among the many exercises taking place at that time were firing practices at various locations, and the awful thought was raised . . . had the donkeys been shot? I recall raising the matter with the Senior British Officer who assured me that they were in no way responsible, with I have to say a very straight face. Here you are preparing to go to war and there's this civilian type worrying about donkeys! In due course when things had quietened down they reappeared, but the whereabouts of their hideaway remained a mystery.

Throughout all of this my major concern was the supply of drinking water. There is very little fresh water on the island and for the British residents, desalinated sea-water is produced by the BBC power station; the Americans have a similar arrangement for their needs. We had a number of storage tanks that held about 30 days supply for normal consumption. Our population had more than doubled and in consequence our evaporation type desalination plants were working flat out. This type of plant requires frequent maintenance and we could ill afford to take them out of service unless absolutely necessary. Our stocks of water were slowly being depleted and at one point were down to about a week. In order to help reverse this trend, the military supplied a small reverse osmosis plant, which despite being somewhat troublesome in the initial stages, helped to avert the unthinkable, but only just. We were never completely out of the wood and it remained a nagging problem throughout. The other unthinkable was the supply of beer. How the clubs managed to keep up with the demand I will never know, but to the gratitude of all concerned they did somehow. I never saw a figure for the consumption of beer, but it must have been astronomical.

The grape-vine, which was normally very active anyway, went into overdrive. Rumours abounded, from Argentinians about to invade, to all civilian wives and families to be sent home, and the place to be designated a military island. With regard to the latter, this might have come about had it not been for a certain Royal Navy Captain who was in charge of the whole operation. It was our good fortune that he realised that the unique infrastructure of the island would suffer irreparably if the military became too dominant. He vetted all personnel arriving, and if they were not essential to the operation they were sent back, despite the MOD wanting to send out increased numbers. I was told later by a RAF Wing Commander who had spent time sitting next to this gentleman, that he constantly put his career at risk arguing the toss with London. I know this to be true because later that year we hosted a dinner for a visiting army General. He asked me about 'this chap who was in charge and who kept sending people back'.

1982 was the 40th anniversary of the building by the Americans of the airstrip, and the Island Historical Society was already well advanced in preparing for a big celebration. We had set in motion arrangements in the USA to track down any of the original members of the unit which had carried out the work, and to persuade the US military to fly them down. We had also located the pilot of the first aircraft to land, a Fairey Swordfish from a nearby

British escort carrier; he was sheep farming in New Zealand and would be willing to come, 'if someone paid his fare'. Plans were being made to celebrate with many different events and we even considered inviting the US President and the Prime Minister. In retrospect the invitation of these two might have been far more appropriate than we could have imagined. In the event of course none of this happened, although a small celebration arranged by the Americans did take place later in the year. I often ponder on the thought of how different the course of history would have been if the airstrip had never been built.

Two particular pieces of music will always bring back vivid memories of this period. The first concerns the song 'Sailing'. The occasion was a dance organised by the Two Boats Club attended by many of the servicemen. They were soon to 'go south' and the event had a certain farewell feel about it tinged with a little sadness. The evening was a huge success and we finished up with an incredibly robust rendition of 'Sailing', complete with the ritual waving of upheld arms, and the effect was quite overwhelming. For my wife and me that song has never been quite the same since.

The other memory occurred on the eve of the Task Force leaving for the Falkland Islands. The Band of Her Majesty's Royal Marines had come ashore to Beat The Retreat on the sports ground, which of course was originally the Marines parade ground dating back to the early 1800's, a fact which gave the evening a certain historical flavour. The band gave its usual immaculate performance, and the Georgetown Exiles Club, which overlooks the sports ground, was absolutely packed to the gills. I cannot recall another occasion when so many were present at the club, and as people continued to arrive several of us became concerned that the balcony, and those of us who occupied it, might not safely survive the night. The resulting babble of conversation and general hubbub was well up the decibel scale for sure. Most of those present were of course members of the services, and we were all well aware that if war was not averted, then many of them might not return. To say that this added a certain poignancy to the evening would be a masterly understatement. Many of us were gathered on the end of the balcony overlooking the sports ground admiring the Marine's performance, and with the daylight fading the band began to play 'Sunset', the customary piece played every evening at sea as the Colours are lowered for the day. This is a somewhat emotive piece of music at the best of times, but on that particular evening emotions were running pretty high, and to add to that, the noise in the club suddenly abated; the sense of occasion was intense, and one which I shall never forget. Of course in the event, war was not averted, and I wonder how many present that night were amongst those who sadly did not return. Ever since, 'Sunset' has had a particularly special association.

Following the departure of the Task Force, two new people joined the community of Two Boats village along with the tools of their trades. They were of far-eastern origin, I never discovered precisely where they came from, and both were off one of the ships having decided not to continue south. (They were employed as civilians on board) One was a cobbler and the other a tailor, and as you can imagine, in no time they became extremely popular, particularly when the ladies found that they could have a dress designed from just a magazine picture; and made up in no time at all!

One of our fortnightly business lunches held by the heads of organisations had been constantly interrupted with private messages for the Administrator and the US Base Commander; clearly something important was going on. Later that evening, our neighbour, the Base Commander, drove past our house in uncharacteristic haste and I guessed en-route for the airstrip. We headed for Command Hill and there we could see the reason. It was the evening that the RAF mounted their first incredible air-to-air refuelling mission to get a Vulcan bomber over Stanley. The lights at the airstrip had been extinguished but we could make out the aircraft lining up at the end of the runway. With engines revving, the noise created by the two Vulcan bombers and a string of Victor tankers was considerable. One by one they took off, each one going as soon as the previous aircraft was airborne. The noise rose to an almost unbearable level as the jets in turn fully opened their throttles for take off. In particular the noise of the tankers with full load seemed to rip the very air. It was an incredible sight that made our adrenalin flow, but not I suspect as much as those involved, theirs must have been on full bore. At the time we could only guess at their destination, but it was clear that wherever it was they meant business. The following day we went down to check if they had all returned safely, and we were glad to see them.

Soon after the dreadful loss of HMS *Sheffield*, it was announced that the survivors would be passing through Ascension on their way back to the UK. They were to arrive early in the morning and would not be leaving until midnight, and families were asked if they would be willing to host them for the day. We were to give them a quiet comfortable day and above all not to talk about their experiences. We hosted three crew members, one of whom was a very young lad for whom *Sheffield* was his first ship - he had apparently joined as a boy seaman. His companions who were both mature seamen were very protective toward him, and hardly surprising considering the effect that such a dreadful event could have on someone so young. They enjoyed the comfortable domestic surroundings and some 'home cooking', which must have been an incredible contrast to their recent horrific experiences. What surprised us most was their desire to talk of almost nothing else but the loss of their ship, and we began to appreciate just what that meant to them. What upset them most was that in naval exercises they said they nearly always came out top of their class, but in this instance they had not had the time to fire a single shot in anger before being taken out. That afternoon we took them to the top of Green Mountain where we found a number of other members of their crew including their Captain 'Sam' Salt. We admired the genuine display of respect these men had for him; they may have lost their ship but not their spirits. We parted company that night hoping that we had helped them in a very small way.

Some of our experiences on Ascension at that particular time certainly made us feel proud of our armed forces, but others brought home to us the horrors of war and the suffering that human beings endure in carrying it out. Oh that we could avoid such things.

Chapter 13

A RESIDENT'S PERSPECTIVE

by Miss Celia James

———

When I was asked to think back to 1982 on Ascension Island during the Falkland Islands crisis , I found my memory disjointed and blurred. How had I felt? What were the important issues for me? It was no good, I just could not put anything together without finding the letters I had sent home during that time and which my mother had thoughtfully saved. A rummage in the loft produced not just those letters but many more – sitting there on the bare boards amongst the dust and beams, I was soon transported back to my beloved Ascension Island.

I had been on Ascension for about a year when the Argentinians decided to invade the Falklands. As I recall we didn't have much to do with those islands other than appreciating that they were not too far away, relatively speaking. I was teaching the Reception Class at Ascension Island School and the services on the island were organised by Cable and Wireless at that time. Being an 'island' lover, I had taken to Ascension immediately. I loved its beautiful, stark, wild beauty – the volcanic terrain, the cones and craters, the incredible colours enhanced by the glorious sunlight. The sun shone every day but there was always a cooling breeze. I loved the white sand beaches, crashing rollers and jet-black volcanic rocks but best of all, I loved the wildlife. The cardinals and mynahs, the frigate birds and boobies and the annual arrival of the Wideawake (sooty) terns and of course the intriguing land crabs and green turtles who came ashore to lay their eggs.

Life was incredibly good until that fateful day in April when it all began in those islands across the ocean – I enjoyed being part of an island community, free from television, a place where we made our own entertainment both outdoors on the beaches in the beach huts or at the central meeting place in Georgetown, the Exiles Club with its balcony overlooking the sea, where you signed vouchers for drinks or helped yourself on trust, if Reggie was not behind the Bar to serve you. I loved the children at the school, mostly St Helenian, they were totally unsophisticated and free as the air since there was no crime on the island. I was also having a wonderful relationship with Don Coffey who was the Base Manager at the USAF Base on the island. We loved to walk together exploring the remote parts of the island at the weekends.

In a letter to my mother is dated April 13th – and headed 'Ascension Island or should I say Military Base now' I begin with the words:

> It is with very mixed feelings that I sit down to write this letter – I would never have believed that two weeks could have altered my entire life here so dramatically and in fact altered the whole tone of the island. It is as if we have been invaded ourselves, except of course it on a friendly basis.

The main thread throughout my letters home from this date onwards is the inadequacy and uselessness of the British who were in charge on the island – the company directors, etc. I was humiliated that we seemed unable and unwilling to offer the help the Forces needed so desperately. I was so proud of the role that Don was playing – the support from our American friends seemed overwhelming and I remember writing to the *Daily Telegraph* about how grateful we should be to the Americans for all they were doing for our soldiers, airmen and Navy personnel at this vital staging post on their way down to the Falklands.

The single people on the island lived together in a large block known as the F1 Mess in Georgetown. Each person had an en-suite room and as the Mess President, I had a delightful flat with a kitchen and a balcony which overlooked the bay and Long Beach. In my letter, I mention the fury I felt when I heard that Ron Field (the head of Cable and Wireless at the time) wanted to charge a fortune for Navy personnel to occupy the many unused rooms in the Mess and also that he had told the officers that as the Mess president, *I* was not keen on them being there – in fact it had been my suggestion that the vacant rooms be given to the Forces since there was very little spare accommodation on the island. Of course in any new situation there are good things and bad.

At first, I was incredibly excited that Ascension was so involved in the War – to see all those famous ships in the Bay, to watch the helicopters from my balcony, helicopters which Don had informed me arrived in pieces, were put together on the airstrip and then flown, backwards and forwards carrying arms and guns and food in nets slung beneath them out to the waiting ships. It was wonderful to meet so many fine men. The officers who shared the Mess were so thoughtful, concerned about the disruption to the island and respectful of our way of life. I was proud of the way we were going to the aid of the Falkland Islanders.

The island was shaken from its sleepy indolence and suddenly launched into a War zone – but suddenly I found fresh vegetables, cauliflowers and cabbages, mushrooms and other delights left outside my flat door, a present from the catering officer – food we only saw rarely when the Charter flight arrived every three months or when the RMS *St Helena* docked! But as the weeks went on my feelings became ambiguous. I began to tire of the constant noise, the curtailment of my freedom to wander all over the island, I hated the Exiles club always filled with loud men. The residents were so much part of the situation and yet the islanders were kept on the periphery – we didn't know what was happening at the airstrip – there were no-go areas everywhere. I began to worry about the effects on the wildlife – the sooty terns had just arrived to begin their breeding cycle on the Fairs beyond the airstrip and immediately in front of them, someone had authorised a shooting range. I couldn't go and check on their welfare. Soldiers were training and 'yomping' all over the island and disturbing the turtles on the beaches at night. I was resentful of the time Don was spending at the Base – I only saw him briefly and then he was so tired, he'd fall asleep in the chair as soon as he arrived. He seemed to be loving every minute of it! I remember feeling guilty – how selfish I was being and how important his work was.

Captain McQueen apologised to me one night at the Club for monopolising Don. Then, one evening, Don took me with him in his truck up to a hillside that overlooked the airstrip, just so I could see what was happening. I was amazed. The strip was covered with pile upon pile of boxes and cartons, guns, pieces of equipment, half built helicopters and lined up were the fighter planes, Harriers and Nimrods I think. Suddenly it was all real, we were at War and it was then I realised that we might even be vulnerable ourselves to an attack. Suppose the Argentinians sent submarines to attack the vast fuel tanks – our island could be blown up. Anxiety also began to creep into my unhappy thoughts.

I was also concerned about the general behaviour of the 'troops' – I found young men trying to go the wrong way up one-way roads, also wandering about the island, shirts off, half naked, due to the heat – this was an embarrassment to the St Helenians who were 'old fashioned' and respectful in their outlook. I wrote of my concerns to the Head of operations – I must have seemed to be a prude but I gather my letter was read out at their evening meeting. I felt pleased that concern was still being shown for the islanders when there were obviously so many other more important things to concern these officers.

One day at school, in the middle of lessons I received a phone call. It was from UK and the school secretary thought it might be important so I was called from class. It turned out to be a journalist from London – how had she got my name? The husband of a 'friend' of mine back in England had mentioned that he knew someone who was working on Ascension Island in the school – he had rung my mother to ask for my number and she, unwittingly had given to him thinking that my friend was wanting to call me. It was only later that she thought it might be for an ulterior motive and she spent a sleepless night worrying about it. The exchange on the island knew I would not be at home and had transferred the call to school! As soon as I knew it was a journalist, I was on my guard, she began probing – what was going on there? "I have no idea," I said, "we are not allowed anywhere near the operations"

"Can you give me some names of personnel?" she asked. "No," I said firmly. "What is the name of your local newspaper and can you give me the phone number of the press photographer", she probed further. Press photographer? I smiled inwardly and passed on Jean Shacklady's number – the Editor of our weekly *Islander* newspaper. I knew she would make mincemeat of any upstart journalist out for a sensational scoop! Her last question however set alarm bells ringing in my mind – "Is Galtieri being held captive on Ascension?" I cut short the phone call by saying I was sorry I had to return to my children. I felt very uneasy about the conversation and talked to Don about it. He reassured me that our island was safe. Later that day, I heard that we would not be allowed to phone UK or receive phone calls from home.

April 24th . . . I wrote home in great excitement because I had had one of those truly 'memorable for all time' moments. I write in my letter:

> I just had to write about this incident NOW, as I am afraid if I don't, parts of it will fade from my memory – how proud my Pa would have been to know where I went last evening! GUESS where I was last night!

I had been invited as Don's 'lady' together with Bill Bryden and Marylou (the Base Commander and his wife) and Bernard Pauncefoot, the Island

Administrator and his wife to dinner on board HMS *Fearless*. I continue in my letter:

Oh, I just get goose pimples thinking about it now – such an honour for me and so EXCITING. I am so glad I am not shy anymore! (can you believe that once I was incredibly shy!!!) I felt completely at ease with the Commodore and the Brigadier and the Wing Commander, the Captain and the Doctor who is in charge of all the medical services of the exercise – a Captain too as he had all the stripes with red in between!

Here is a copy of the invitation:

Commodore M.C. Clapp and Brigadier J.H.A. Thompson request the pleasure of the company of Mr Don Coffey and Lady to dinner on board HMS *Fearless* at 19.00 for 19.30 on Friday 23rd April 1982.

Transport by helicopter will leave Wideawake at 18.55. Ladies are requested to wear trousers for the helicopter flight. Facilities to change will be provided.

Dress – casual.

Casual? How could such an occasion be casual? I was ready at 5 pm – I remember I had a good tan and wore a white dress with bare shoulders and a new necklace made from white pieces of mother of pearl shell made on Ascension by an American! Don drove us out to the airstrip where once again, I mention how overwhelming all the activity was there.
I continue:

They gave us life jackets and ear muffs as the noise was deafening – then off we went, ducking under the whirring blades of a Sea King helicopter – they literally lifted me aboard and I sat near the open door and just in front of a little window – there was just the pilot and another chap who hung out of the door all the time – he was attached to a life line inside the helicopter – above the door was a rail with little hooks on (for parachutes?) and in the doorway, a stand for a gun. I think seeing all these things has really brought it home to me what is happening and how incredibly *serious* it all is. I only regret that I did not see all this earlier and appreciate Don's important role. There was a sort of shudder and a jerk sideways and suddenly the ground looked far away and all the marshallers and people on the apron very tiny – we were off!! We flew out to sea and along the coast line – how wonderful to see Ascension from the air bathed in evening sunlight! We flew over the Base and Georgetown and I could pick every out all the houses so clearly – it was so exciting but seemed over in five minutes! Then we were hovering over a ship in the bay – I could see *Canberra* just to the side of us – we came down lower and lower and seemed to be sinking into the bowels of the ship and then there was just a little bump and we were on the apron bit, surrounded by various bits of equipment for War – a sharp reminder again. We jumped down from the helicopter and were introduced to the Captain and the Commodore and some other young officers. Then we were ushered through various parts of the ship – up and down stairs and along corridors piled high with stores – it all looked a bit disorganised until I learnt they had had to leave in a huge hurry – only three days to make ready rather than seven. We – the ladies – were shown into a very nicely furnished cabin with floral covers on the chairs and a small bedroom and bathroom attached – there were pictures on the wall and a television and video – all very homely. I think it was the Brigadier's cabin as his green beret was on the dressing table!

We all got changed – my hair was an abomination as usual due to the wind and ear-muffs! Then one of the young ratings took us to a tiny room with a bar and we had pre-dinner drinks. I talked to the Commodore at first and then I met the Captain who was very tall and lean and rangey – he was all for organising a party for the whole school on board if they are still here on Wednesday – how wonderful for the children! Then I chatted to the Brigadier – a small man but with eyes like two drills. I felt he wasn't one for small talk! No wonder – I think he is Head of the Commandos.

Soon we went into dinner – the dining room was beautiful – polished wood, cut glass and silver with wonderful prints on the wall. I was seated next to the Medical officer and opposite the Wing Commander from the RAF who was a super chap and seemed incredibly young for such a rank. The doctor was super to talk to and I had a really fascinating evening – he actually knew what a Norland Nurse was (I am a Norland Nurse as well as a teacher!) The Brigadier was talking about Brunei so I told him I had spent two years in North Borneo. I hardly appreciated what I was eating because I was so involved in conversation! Time passed so quickly – I wanted to stop it all and freeze it so it would last for ever – I was feeling so happy!

After the red wine with the main course – the Port and the Madeira came round – Bill Bryden just passed the decanter to me but I knew I should not pour it myself so just waited – the kind Doctor leaned across and saved me! Then Captain Robert McQueen stood up and toasted the President of the United States and then Bill Bryden stood up and toasted the Queen. After that we adjourned to a little room for coffee and liqueurs.

All too soon we had to go as our helicopter had arrived – we crept down black stairways in the pitch dark after changing back into our trousers – the Captain took us down into the hold. *Fearless* is an AMAZING ship – do you know it is so ingenious, it can sink itself and release boats from the hold right into the sea and they can sail back in that way too – incredible! We said our goodbyes and were rushed over to the helicopter – I looked back and felt suddenly very tearful – perhaps I would never see some of these super men again – they were going to War – they might be killed. It was all becoming more and more REAL.

This really has been one of the most exhilarating and exciting days of my entire life! We went to the Exiles then for a celebratory bottle of champagne – it's my anniversary. One year on Ascension – what a way to celebrate!

In other letters, I talk about a wonderful flight with the children from my class in a Chinook helicopter and also make special note of the incredible buildings Don organised for the troops – designed for their rapid deployment forces. Concertina City – buildings which come as a flat pack in a box which open out like a concertina and have folded beds and loos and chairs neatly stowed inside –there are power points and linen and bedding immediately ready for the men to move into in just two hours! There are even brooms and brushes and squeegee mops and curtains and compartments to keep things in! It can all be folded away again after use. How very clever. There are even shower units and field kitchen units and a laundry unit – all flat-packed the same! They can even be jacked up onto uneven ground.

So, life on Ascension was never the same again – after the War was over there was much activity with the building of a larger apron and improvements to the runway at the airstrip and the construction of the RAF camp. This provided the residents with some wonderful new facilities that we were allowed to use, but it meant that we never returned to those dreamy halcyon days before it all began. Ascension had become so much more than an insignificant speck on the world map in the middle of the South Atlantic Ocean.

Chapter 14

PERCEPTIONS OF COMMANDING OFFICER 3RD COMMANDO BRIGADE

by Major General Julian Thompson CB RM

The first troops of the 3rd Commando Brigade to arrive at Ascension Island were X Company, 45 Commando, Royal Marines, who flew in, followed shortly afterwards by Y Company. Both companies bivouacked near English Bay, a small cove that would just accept one Landing Craft Utility (LCU). This was a large landing craft capable of taking up to two main battle tanks, or five four-ton trucks or 20 troops. The two companies carried out training and as Captain Gardiner, commanding X Company, wrote later, 'We enjoyed our stay . . . The position was sufficiently chaotic for people to be glad not to be interested in us. So we conducted ourselves largely to our own satisfaction and completed the most worthwhile training programme I think I have ever seen.'

The remainder of the Brigade arrived at Ascension by sea over a number of days, in sixteen ships. The Brigade, normally consisting of three Royal Marine Commandos, a Commando Gunner Regiment, a Commando Logistic Regiment, Engineers, light helicopters, and supporting arms, had been greatly expanded by the addition of two parachute battalions and other units so that it eventually consisted of about 5,500 men in eight major units and fifteen minor ones. No training areas or ranges existed on the island. However, Mr Coffey the PanAm manager at Ascension came on board HMS *Fearless* the day that the Brigade Commander arrived with his headquarters, and said that he had instructions from his boss in the USA to provide all possible assistance. He suggested areas that could be used for live firing and provided empty oil drums to be used as targets, these and other facilities provided by him were invaluable. He combined a special experience that enabled him to set up five ranges on the island without affecting the local wild life. His experience in the US Special Forces in Vietnam meant that he understood the military requirement completely and his love and knowledge of the island and its wildlife meant that he knew how to integrate the ranges with the least effect on the wildlife. He was partnered by Major (now Colonel) Hector Gullan who helped Don with reconnoitring the ranges and setting up the targets.

Apart from planning, there were three requirements for the Landing and Amphibious Task Groups at this stage, all demanding ship-shore movement assets (helicopters, landing craft and mexeflotes): amphibious training, trials and work-up; cross-decking of vehicles, equipment and stores; and taking troops ashore for training.

Cross decking and re-stow

The normal practice when conducting an amphibious operation is to stow your ships after you have made your plan based on intelligence and other factors. In this way you achieve 'combat loading', so troops and equipment offload in the right sequence. Lacking a contingency plan for an operation to re-take the Falkland Islands, and in the rush to sail from the UK, there had not been enough time or intelligence to make a plan and combat load the ships. Some ships arrived at Ascension grossly overloaded, for example many of the Landing Ships Logistics (LSLs) which were up to eighteen inches over their loading marks. Some ships, such as *Canberra*, arrived with space to spare. In others, there were highly dangerous mixtures of loads, such as packed fuel and ammunition in one space. One LSL diverted from Belize totally empty. The staffs of 3rd Commando Brigade and Commodore Clapp quickly produced a re-stow plan; that was the straight-forward part.

The re-stow at Ascension Island would have been far easier and accomplished in less than the twelve days it took, had there been a port with slipways to accept Ro-Ro ferries and LSLs and room to unload most of the vehicles and stores. There was no port. The operation was conducted at anchor in Georgetown Roads, which is subject to the ceaseless mid-Atlantic swell, deceptively smooth when viewed from the deck of a large ship, or from ashore, but demanding great skill on the part of coxswains of landing craft and Mexeflotes. Mexeflotes are the large floats carried by LSLs to carry stores and vehicles. These were heaving up and down at the stern ramps and bow doors of Ro-Ros and LSLs, while vehicles were gingerly edged on or off; or alongside, with ships' cranes plumbed over the side dangling loaded trucks or light tanks (Combat Vehicles Reconnaissance Tracked (CVRT)). The logisticians had to play a complex puzzle game, the movement of one 'piece'; truck or equipment from ship to ship almost invariably required several other 'pieces' to be moved first. All over the anchorage, floating 'parks' of vehicles and stores on Mexeflotes could be seen bobbing in the swell, while they waited their turn to come to the ship, or ships, to deliver their loads and take more.

Round-the-clock working was not possible since landing craft crews needed to get some rest. Furthermore, the sighting of an Argentine freighter off the island gave rise to the assessment, spurious as it turned out, that she might have landed frogmen to attack ships in the anchorage. From that time on ships put to sea at night.

Helicopters were employed for the lighter and more accessible loads, but their use was restricted by four considerations. First, they were in short supply. Second, there was a need to conserve engine hours against the day when helicopters would be needed for the assault landing in the Falklands, and subsequent tactical and logistical tasks. Third, they were in demand for

Cross-decking by Mexeflote

rehearsals and trials. Fourth, they were needed to transfer stores flown out from UK to Ascension to ships in the anchorage.

Amphibious training, trials and work-up

None of the training or work-up included a full-scale rehearsal of the Brigade landing plan in darkness, as recommended by the manuals, based on experience in two World Wars. Even a 'turn away' landing, normally regarded as the bare minimum, was impossible because of the demands on craft and helicopters and shortage of time.

The first task facing the staffs was to test and work up the various elements of the Amphibious and Landing Force Task Groups. None of the merchant ships and many of the RFAs (except the LSLs) had ever been involved in amphibious operations. Some of the troops, most notably the two parachute battalions and other army units not normally part of the 3rd Commando Brigade were equally new to the art.

A number of procedures had to be worked out from first principles. Space does not permit a full list, but the example of *Canberra* will give a flavour of the many problems posed by the need to carry out an amphibious assault from ships that have not been designed for such an operation, or modified as was done extensively in the Second World War. How for example, do you transfer a battalion of heavily laden troops, in the dark, in a seaway, into LCUs alongside a cruise liner? What assault routes within *Canberra* need to be practised, so that men loaded with rucksacks arrive at the loading point with their weapons, ammunition, grenades, mortar bombs, anti-tank missiles, and other impedimenta? Should the ship be at anchor, lying still, or steaming slowly ahead? How long would it take would it take ten Sea King helicopters landing two at a time, one on each of the two spots on Canberra to lift a company group, form up into a wave, and land them? Only because the Brigade and Commodore's staff had years of amphibious expertise at their fingertips, could they arrive at answers to these and a myriad other problems needing to be resolved.

The best possible compromise between demands on craft and helicopters for re-stowing ships, for trials, working up and training, resulted in one helicopter training day for each commando or battalion and artillery battery; and a day and night landing session for each commando and battalion. Each commando, battalion and battery was allocated one day ashore to fire its weapons. The exceptions were 2nd Battalion The Parachute Regiment (2 Para), and T Air Defence Battery RA, the Rapier battery.

2 Para arrived in the *Norland* on the day the Amphibious Task Group was due to sail south from Ascension. There was time for only a daytime rehearsal with landing craft. This lack of night training was evident in the Amphibious Operating Area on the night of D-Day 21st May 1982, when failure by the *Norland* to carry out the correct drills, including dropping one soldier between the ship and the craft, resulted in such slow embarkation of troops into the LCUs that H-Hour had to be delayed. 2 Para did not carry out any training ashore either.

T Battery had just landed at Ascension to fire at drone targets specially flown out from UK, accompanied by instructors from Larkhill, when the HQ at Northwood threw a spanner in the works by demanding that the Amphibious Task Group sail at once. All troops were withdrawn from training ashore. The Commodore eventually persuaded them to change their minds, mainly on the grounds that the Group was in the middle of the re-stow and the state of loads was worse than when ships left UK. By the time this episode had been successfully resolved, the opportunity to land T Battery was lost. The lack of practice was to be evident on D-Day.

Training ashore
Because of the dust ingestion problem, helicopters could land only on the airfield, which was so busy that only the two non-tactical helicopter landing practices mentioned above could be carried out because these required the airfield to be closed to other traffic. The training ashore was confined to zeroing personal weapons and firing support weapons: mortars, general purpose machine guns (GPMGs), shoulder fired anti-tank weapons 84 mm Carl Gustav and 66 mm LAW in the sustained fire role, MILAN wire-guided anti-tank weapons and Mobat 120 mm recoilless guns. Here the ranges found for us by Mr Don Coffey proved so valuable.

Training ammunition, flown out from UK, was unusually plentiful; for example, 3rd Battalion the Parachute Regiment fired about twelve years training allocation of High Energy Squash Head (HESH) in one day at Ascension. At least one Commando took the opportunity to fire its MILANs with High Energy Anti Tank (HEAT) warheads; these are not usually available for peacetime training.

The Ranges
No 1 Range was a small arms range in English Bay for 7.62 mm, SLR, GPMG, 9 mm SMG and Pistol. It enabled all the troops to zero their weapons.

No 2–4 Ranges were south west of Wideawake, reaching 12 km out to sea and up to 20,000 ft They were for 66 mm LAW, 84 mm Carl Gustav, Milan, GPMG – SF, 81 mm Mortar and Mobat 120 mm. They were adjacent to but clear of the bird sanctuary. The story is told of four Sea Harriers joining the Wideawake circuit. As they ran in the ranges were closed and as the fourth aircaft touched down the ranges were reopened. Such was the co-operation and control.

No 5 Range was the Crater Range stretching south east from SE Crater 17,000 km out to sea. This was for 105 mm artillery, 81 mm Mortar and Blowpipe.

A sixth range for live Rapier firings was prepared but not activated since the Amphibious Task Force was sailed before it was possible to position T Battery.

Problems with stores arriving by air from UK
One immediate logistic problem that arose involved the stream of stores pouring into Ascension Island for the 3rd Commando Brigade in response to signalled demands. The problem was caused by the lack of any Ordnance Corps personnel at Ascension to 'recognise' the item and arrange for helicopter transport to the correct recipient. As stores arrived, they piled up and were not distributed to the units concerned for two reasons. First, if the item was addressed to a particular unit, there was no one ashore on Ascension who knew on which ship, or ships, the addressee was embarked (some units were embarked on several ships). Second, if as often happened, there was only a demand number on the package, the party in Ascension was even more perplexed. The standard reaction in either case was usually to do nothing, or at a pinch despatch the item to a ship, any ship. Some ships that had no landing force units embarked were surprised to receive equipment and parts whose purpose was a total mystery to them.

At the request of 3rd Commando Brigade, an ordnance team was flown from the UK to sort out the problem. Without reference to the Brigade, the team was sent back to UK on the grounds that there was insufficient accommodation and water on the island. Eventually, to cope with the distribution of stores for units of the 3rd Commando Brigade, a team from the Ordnance Squadron in the Commando Logistic Regiment was landed each day until the Amphibious Group sailed. They could be ill spared from the task of supervising the re-stow of ships. Their efforts restored order to what had become a chaotic situation, but not before some stores had gone missing completely. These included special ammunition and weapons intended for the Brigade Reconnaissance Troop, which were appropriated by an SAS Squadron passing through Ascension *en route* to South Georgia, who, seeing them lying around, had taken a fancy to them. More were sent out, but arrived after the Amphibious Group had sailed.

The Task Force Commander's Council of War at Ascension
The Task Force Commander, Admiral Sir John Fieldhouse, C-in-C Fleet, took the opportunity to fly in by RAF VC-10 to Ascension Island on 17th April, to meet all three Task Group Commanders gathered in HMS *Hermes*, and hold a what is best described as a 'council of war'. No orders were issued at this session, but a number of misunderstandings and misconceptions were resolved. The Task Force Commander also addressed the COs of ships at Ascension, in the wardroom of the *Hermes*. Among the points he made was the need for COs to impress upon their ships companies that they might well be going to war, and for many of them this would be a chance to earn the pay they had received over the years from the British taxpayer. Those present at the address who had previously been on operations during their service took note.

On two other occasions, staff from Task Force Headquarters in Northwood, took the opportunity to visit the commanders of the Amphibious and Landing Force Groups by RAF flight to Ascension. Of these the most important was the visit by Major General Jeremy Moore, the Land Deputy to Admiral Fieldhouse. Commodore Clapp and Brigadier Thompson briefed General Moore on their preferred landing plan in the Falkland Islands, with a beachhead at San Carlos. General Moore returned to UK with this plan. It was cleared by the Task Force Commander, and eventually by the Chiefs of Staff. It was this plan that was put into effect on D-Day, 21st May 1982. This face-to-face meeting was invaluable, and a considerable improvement on conducting such important discussions by signal or by the almost un-intelligible SATCOM telephone.

Chapter 15

Ubique – The Sappers Were There

by Colonel Peter Hill, Royal Engineers

———

Go to Ascension Island and report to the RN Captain in command. He is not convinced he needs Sapper support and will probably try to send you back. Your job is to convince him otherwise and reinforce the infrastructure of the island to cope with being a major naval and air force base. Here is the reconnaissance report identifying your tasks. Whatever you do, do not get sent back.

This was the briefing given to a Sapper major, who at the time had just started a posting as an instructor teaching the practicalities of reinforced concrete design to post-degree RE officers. The long Tri-Star flight to Ascension provided plenty of time to study the report and to try to work out why the MoD had selected a specialist civil engineer to deal with problems that seemed to be mainly mechanical and electrical. The reconnaissance report had been prepared by a team from the Military Works Force led by Brigadier 'Jungly' Drake and was extremely thorough, setting out what needed to be done in some detail. The report was almost an idiot's guide, which could explain why the MoD had concluded that it was not necessary to send an officer with the appropriate specialist skills but this thought did nothing to boost confidence. The welcome at Wideawake Airfield was guarded and it was made very clear that anyone considered non-essential would be on the next plane back.

Fortunately, there was an urgent problem to deal with. The existing aviation fuel system depended on road tankers ferrying the fuel from bulk storage tanks fed by a ship-to-shore line to a small tank farm on the airfield. The road tankers could not move the fuel fast enough and the road was beginning to break up. The solution was to lay a 3-mile pipeline from the shore installation to a flexible tank farm on the airfield. This meant connecting in to the US fuel systems at both ends and therefore a government-to-government agreement on who would be responsible for any damage. A typewriter was located and an agreement prepared and signed on the spot. The US copy was reported to have been sent to Washington to be laid before Congress; the UK's version was filed in a convenient cardboard box acting as the British Forces Support Unit filing cabinet.

Pipes, pumps and pipeline accessories began to arrive, as did a Troop from 51 Squadron Royal Engineers to provide the muscle power. The first task was to play 'hunt the pipeline stores' in the stores dump on the airfield, as there was no warning of how and when these would arrive. Fortunately, advice on identification was on hand from the Military Works Force bulk petroleum team and all the stores were located. The pipeline route could not run alongside the road in case it was damaged by vehicles so the muscle power of the Sapper troop had to be used to clear obstructions and move the pipes into position by hand across the rugged terrain of ash and lava fields. The hard physical work in the Ascension Island sun persuaded some Sappers to strip to the waist despite warnings of sunburn. They were quickly dissuaded by finding that the standard treatment given by the local nurse was to paint the burnt area with iodine. That she was one of the few single females on the island was little compensation for the stinging pain and the rush to get a tan stopped dead.

The pipeline and pillow tanks were laid and connected and after the usual problems of starting up pumps that had been taken straight from the UK's war reserve, aviation fuel began to flow. At first, pump performance was patchy and the road tankers had to be kept in service but after a few days reliability improved to the point of being able to use the pipeline only. This was very welcome news to the Cable and Wireless works group patching up the crumbling road from the shore installation to the airfield.

Accommodation was the next challenge. A tent city had sprung up around the apron on the airfield but without much town planning. Tents had been put up across access routes, generators were upwind of accommodation and the solitary toilet was unable to cope. The airfield apron area was a US facility so it seemed to the Sappers that another government-to-government agreement for new latrines was called for.

Agreement between the United States and the United Kingdom for the construction of trench latrines on Wideawake Airfield, Ascension Island.

The only toilet failed the strain,
for Wideawake Airfield has no drain,
so the British must restrain
their bowels.

The US Government hereby permits
the construction of two septic pits
for UK airmen with the s—ts
on Wideawake.

The UK will the structure build
and when the trenches are quite filled
and before the contents can be spilled,
will seal them.

Signed this the sixth day of July 1982 at Ascension Island

For the Government of the United States	For the Government of the United Kingdom
Colonel USAF Base Commander	Major, Royal Engineers

This agreement probably never reached Washington. The latrines were sited well downwind and probably needed to be, as it was difficult to dig deep enough in the mixture of ash and lava boulders. An electrical power distribution system for the tented camp was established and a bank of generators set up, also downwind. The 40 kVA generators sent out were new in service and had no spares backing. When the electronic speed/voltage regulators started to fail in the heat, more complete generators were airlifted out. These too failed after a few hours running and the next response from the UK was a computer-generated authority to local purchase the necessary spares. Further argument with the computer proved fruitless and it was necessary to forcefully buttonhole a passing VIP visitor and ask for some of the tried and tested 27½ kVA generators now relegated to the war reserve. These came and were installed. After being fitted with new filters and seals and the governors adjusted in the traditional way with a dollop of chewing gum, they worked reliably. Some of the 40 kVAs were later made to work by a RAF electronic technician with time on his hands but the response for such an initiative was a rebuke from UK for making an unauthorised modification.

The tents on the airfield were hot and dusty and were deemed unsuitable for those aircrew who needed to be there. This problem had been identified in the Drake reconnaissance report and some prefabricated flat pack accommodation huts were ordered and flown out. Putting these up posed the same sort of problems but on a far larger scale as assembling an Ikea wardrobe, even though the instructions were written in English. The first hut proved that unless the base was accurately levelled, none of the roof and wall joints would mate. This was corrected and with the assistance of a borrowed crane the huts were assembled, the services connected and, most importantly, the air conditioning units installed. The availability of this accommodation appeared to create a caste system among the air-crew with the C130 crews being exiled to English Bay, where they were made most welcome by the Sapper troop. English Bay was difficult to reach, as transport was scarce and all service drivers were expected to pick up as many hitch-hikers as they could fit in, but was probably the nicest location as it caught the winds and had a swimming beach. The Sappers refurbished the abandoned hutted camp there for themselves and other units. Other empty buildings in Georgetown and in the settlement of Two Boats were also refurbished by re-wiring, re-plumbing and putting back the doors and windows which had been stripped out.

The old stone buildings in Georgetown became popular billets as the thick walls kept them cool and the limited social life was centred in Georgetown. A request from one officer to improve the view from the terrace of his billet by blasting away a rock blocking the view was accepted but only if he was prepared to sit on the rock during its removal. The offer was rejected. For the refurbishment of the houses, the Sappers relied heavily on support from the Cable and Wireless works section and the Superintendent was delighted to get rid of old stock and old tools.

Fresh water was the third infrastructure need. The first inhabitants on the island relied on a dewpond near the summit of Green Mountain. Later a small spring named Dampier's Drip was found and a pipeline laid to bring the water to Georgetown. The holding tank above Georgetown is called the God-be-thanked Tank that indicates the importance of this supply at that time. US Army Engineers tried to improve the flow from the Dampier's Drip during WW2 by blasting the rocks around it but only succeeded in blocking the spring and the desalination plant at English Bay became the sole source of fresh water. The capacity of this plant was limited and the levels in the fresh water tanks soon became a matter for report in the daily briefing. A reverse osmosis treatment plant was flown in and installed in parallel with the existing distillation plant. The feed water came from the sea water cooling supply to the power station and contained a considerable amount of sand and silt which tended to block the RO 'candles', despite frequent back flushing. This problem was overcome with extra filtering on the sea water intake and the reliability of the plant then equalled those installed on the ships in the Task Force. The supply of fresh water ceased to be a critical item. A second RO plant was brought in and installed at the US camp. This was 'ruggedised' in-service equipment and had fewer operating problems than the UK plant that had been specially assembled for use on Ascension.

The Sapper troop was the only formed unit on the island, apart from an SAS squadron at the top of Green Mountain rehearsing for an attack which was never launched on Argentinian airfields, and so tended to be called upon when manpower was needed to move stores or provide guards. An alternative solution in the early days was to send out a press-gang to the swimming pool and beaches to pick up 'volunteers'. This netted a wide range of ranks and some banter about callouses destroying the delicate touch needed to operate sophisticated equipment. The SAS squadron did in fact carry out a raid but only to liberate from the clothing store a supply of desert boots, which had been sent out as single-Service issue.

As always, the Sappers quickly integrated with the local population and towards the end of their stay, were able to repay hospitality with some community works. The largest of these was for a replacement bridge at Banana Ravine on 'Cronk's Path', cut into the side of Green Mountain in 1921 for the then Superintendent of the Island Farm. At last, a job for a civil engineer but the only material available was scrap metal so that the design had to be simple rather than elegant. The bridge was prefabricated and lifted into position by the RAF Chinook as it was too heavy for the RN helicopters. Afterwards, the pilot admitted that this had been one of his most hair-raising moments as the wind was gusting unpredictably and the blade tips almost touched the mountainside. Perhaps the stay of the Sappers can best be summed up by this letter to 'The Islander', Ascension Island's weekly news sheet (price 15p in 1982):

Dear Editor

ENGINEERS ESCAPE ASCENSION

The Royal Engineers on Ascension Island would like to say farewell and thank you to the many friends we have made here. We came to stay for 10 days to build a pipeline but have found enough to do to have kept us here 3 months. We leave the island a new bridge at Banana Ravine in return for having 'borrowed' some of the old pipes. We nearly left a Sapper as well under the rockfall behind Garden Cottage but, though a little dented, he comes back with us. We would have liked to take away the Georgetown pillar box as a souvenir but have only taken it as far as the Cable and Wireless yard for repainting.

There is a lot we would like to do but Sappers are in short supply. No doubt we shall be passing through Ascension next year en route to Port Stanley so perhaps it is au revoir rather than good bye. Any chance of sending the PSA south so that we could come back to Ascension instead?

Yours sincerely,

The Royal Engineers.

Responsibility for infrastructure support was handed over to the Property Services Agency when the Sappers left.

Chapter 16

ASCENSION ISLAND REVISITED

by Miss Cecilia James

———

Faint as the first pencil marks on a sketch, the craggy outline of Green Mountain emerged from the clouds above the Atlantic ocean – its familiar shape brought hot tears to my eyes conflicting with the cold thrill I was feeling as I returned to my beloved Ascension Island. It had been fifteen years since I left in 1985 – now I was seated in the cockpit, courtesy of the Captain, as the RAF Tristar descended to Wideawake airstrip. No wonder I was overwhelmed with emotion.

As I climbed down the steps from the plane into bright sunlight and felt that warm balmy wind – it really seemed as if I was returning home. Arrival formalities were completed and there was my old friend Don Coffey to meet me.

My first impression of the island was astounding – it rained! In fact showers were quite frequent, and as a result the island is now much greener with vegetation descending from the slopes of Green Mountain across the once barren clinker plains below. I found several favourite walks completely overgrown and impenetrable due to the increase in vegetation and regular pathways barred by rock falls and earth slips.

Over the next two weeks I found many changes. The hardest part was being regarded by most of the expatriate community as an outsider, but I was reassured when I was instantly recognised and welcomed by many Saint Helenian friends who had remained on the island. I delighted in finding my little pupils matured into young adults with good jobs working for the RAF or on the American Base.

Georgetown looked relatively unchanged, though many of the buildings had changed usage. The F1 Mess had become the Georgetown Guesthouse, the large sitting room downstairs, renowned as a venue for the wildest parties, was now the tourist office. My little flat with the wonderful view from the balcony over Georgetown and Long Beach was advertised in the glossy brochure as the VIP suite! Cars for hire were parked in the forecourt. The Exiles Club had suffered most – originally the hub of social life in Georgetown, it had reflected the ethos of the island, ever open with an 'on trust' system of vouchers for members. I was horrified therefore to find the staircase barred at the top with an iron gate and padlock.

I returned to the school and was saddened to find pupil numbers much diminished – only four children in the reception class. On the road to Green Mountain, the hairpin bends (ramps) seemed just as alarming. At the top, the farm and cottages were completely overgrown and decaying, there were problems with the water supply to the cottages caused by someone's carelessness. I remembered cool, refreshing weekends there away from the enervating heat of Georgetown. There was a overwhelming aura of apathy, neglect and disinterest. It reduced me to tears.

Overall there seemed to be fewer people on the island. The RAF personnel numbers were much reduced. The camp's facilities were open to residents for a fee, and provide much needed sporting venues and a wonderful swimming pool. The only safe swimming areas on the beaches remain at English Bay and Comfortless Cove, where I was pleased to see the Bonetta Cemetry preserved and restored.

Despite the changes, the island remains as beautiful and wild as ever. I walked and explored undisturbed, rediscovering all the wildlife I loved. I did become increasingly anxious about the apparent dearth of land crabs until, on my last day, I was caught in a sudden heavy shower. They emerged from under the rocks in their hundreds to dance in the puddles and float gleefully down the streams of water running along the roadside.

Television and video has undoubtedly had a detrimental effect on the sense of community life, which was so vibrant when I lived on the island. The residents had been offered this facility in the 1980s, but we refused it knowing what an impact it would make. The island is now being promoted as a tourist attraction but I feel much needs to be done to improve the facilities first. It can be a dangerous place for the unprepared.

Currently, the evolution continues. Politically, things are changing, with the island becoming a democracy and the possibility of property being for sale. Whatever happens in the future, Ascension Island is ultimately unique.

I will always feel that part of me remains there.

Chapter 17

POSTSCRIPT

———

The Administrator's premonition that the civilian and the military communities 'must come to terms with each other' might leave the reader with the question: how did it all turn out? I shall attempt to answer this question with a short snapshot of how the two communities co-exist today without delving too deeply into the twenty-two years that have elapsed in between.

After the war, the Ministry of Defence decided to build a properly constituted base for the officers and other ranks who were required to man the staging post which continues to exist and will do so for as long as British Forces are required to garrison the Falkland Islands. It was recognised that, in addition to accommodation facilities, proper recreational facilities including a swimming pool were required. The cost of this venture was high (one estimate is £25 million) but it should be remembered that this involved carrying all the materials to the island and bringing them ashore by lighter and crane to Clarence Pier in Georgetown before taking them up the hill to the new Royal Air Force station. This large undertaking was completed in 1984.

By a remarkable coincidence, the number of people on the Island now is very nearly the same (1000) as it was before the war. Because of the cost of supporting people on an island where everything has to be shipped in by sea or air, there is a commercial pressure to have as few people as are really needed. There has been a reduction in the numbers needed by Cable and Wireless and the BBC, the latter having contracted some of their operation to VT Merlin. This has been offset by an increase in the numbers of contractors employed for the MOD task (200 approximately). There are only 33 British and 2 US Service people.

This is a considerable reduction from the RAF numbers in 1997 (165). There has been a welcome increase in the numbers of St Helenians employed by the various contractors. The following facilities have been outsourced: aircraft turnarounds, engineering administration, supply, POL, catering, cleaning, property management, grounds maintenance, water and sewage treatment under the control of a multi-activity contractor. This supports the three flights per fortnight to and from the Falklands Islands (Mount Pleasant Airport).

It can be seen that the number of service people (29 RAF, 4 Army and 2 US) is a very small proportion of the total of 1000. The local community is allowed to use the service facilities such as the gym and the swimming pool (for a small charge to cover insurance). The officers' and sergeants' mess is well supported by a lot of off-base members. The service presence is 'taken for granted' and relationships between the service and civilian communities have to be in harmony. Use of the swimming pool is particularly appreciated since the beautiful beaches on the island are mainly dangerous because of the occasional unusually heavy rollers.

On May 1st 2004, the Royal Air Force handed the base over to the Permanent Joint Headquarters (PJHQ) and it is now known as Ascension Island Base. It comes under the tactical control (TACON) of HQ British Forces South Atlantic Islands (HQ BFSAI) which was previously known as HQ British Forces Falkland Islands (HQ BFFI). It is not known why this has taken so long to happen.

Meanwhile, tourist access to the previously 'closed' island is now available, although an entry permit (£11) has to be obtained from the Administrator. An Ascension Island Council has been appointed as part of the democratic development of the island, which is one of the British Overseas Territories. Up market tourism is encouraged and there is a hotel called The Obsidian owned by a consortium of five local individuals. There is an Ascension Island Works and Services Agency and a Fire and Sea Rescue Service has been set up. There has been talk of taxation of individuals to help pay for island facilities that were previously funded by the organisations using the Island. This is, somewhat naturally, opposed by those who live there. Two conservation officers have been appointed under the auspices of Wildlife Management International. There is an offshore sport fishing boat for four anglers and a savings bank was opened in Georgetown in 1966. The Royal Society for the Protection of Birds (RSPB) has partly funded an initiative to remove the 500 or so feral cats on the island and the Ascension Island Government (AIG) is in the process of increasing its rat control programme in response to the subsequent recent increase in rat numbers!

The author is not qualified to comment on the initiatives towards the democratic development of the island as part of the British Overseas Territories except to recognise the difficulties of this problem.

With all the benefits of hindsight, I am led to the following conclusions. First, the tremendous and wholehearted support for the UK in the Falklands War by the US government and at local level has received scant recognition. In particular, I refer to the timely delivery of the Aim 9L Sidewinder missiles to the Task Force at Ascension, the ever flowing supply of aviation fuel from the US tankers on the fuelling buoy and the supply of the portable accommodation. This book also brings out the close and positive support given beyond the call of duty by Americans and St Helenians alike in the day-to-day support of the Task Force.

Second, contrary to Mr Pauncefort's premonitions, the military base has invigorated the employment situation on the island and the decrease in the size of the workforce of Cable and Wireless and the BBC has been offset by the increase in the numbers employed by the MOD and their contractors. Rapid completion of the base accommodation and recreational facilities quickly lessened the dependency of the services on the locals and the military and civilian societies have remained in harmony. Introduction of contractors has helped this by reducing the numbers of servicemen and providing employment for the St Helenians. The latter outcome is particularly commendable.

Third, the command and control has been rationalised under the PDHQ at last (2004). One hopes that this will prevent a recurrence of the invasion from behind, which we encountered and repelled in 1982. Although the requirement for a staging post for the Falkland Islands air support service looks as if it will be required for the foreseeable future, it is suggested that a recurrence of hostilities is unlikely. But we thought that in 1982!